WARNING!
DATING may be
HAZARDOUS
to your health!

by
Claudette McShane

Published by
Mother Courage Press

This book was made possible in part by a grant from from
the American Association of University Women Educational
Foundation.

The names in this book have been changed to protect the
anonymity of the women who responded to the survey.

Library of Congress Catalog Card Number 88-60718
ISBN 0-941300-08-0

Mother Courage Press
1522 Illinois Street
Racine, WI 53405

To Patrick,
my partner in love and life

Acknowledgments

To the hundreds of women who took time to share their stories with me, I owe the deepest respect and appreciation. Your courage in coming forth with personal accounts of dating abuse fostered the spark needed to complete this book. May you know that other women's lives will be spared pain because of your actions.

I am also greatly indebted to the American Association of University Women Educational Foundation for awarding me a grant to work on this book. Your early trust in what I was doing supported me in ways which far exceeded the generosity of the award.

To my dear friend Elaine who helped in my understanding of dating abuse as a problem affecting women of all ages, thank you for your consistent care and concern.

To Barbara Lindquist and Jeanne Arnold of Mother Courage Press, two women with a vision, I extend my respect for your attention to detail, your integrity and your commitment to this book.

And a special appreciation to Patrick, my husband, for his never-ending belief in me and to my sons, Mark and Ryan, who cooperated with their nap and school schedules.

Contents

Part Two
What Happens,
Who It Happens To and Why

Part Three
The Healing Process

Part Four
Prevention

Dating Abuse:
Private Nightmares Become Public

A middle-aged businessman looked puzzled when I told him that I was writing a book about dating abuse. "But dating is when you put your best foot forward. Why would someone be abusive? It just doesn't make sense." He knew that dating meant social engagements, courtship, going out and having a good time; he understood that abuse signified mistreatment, degradation or injuries. He couldn't comprehend how the two fit together.

A single woman in her late 20s flippantly told me that dating *itself* was an abuse. She was referring facetiously to her still non-married state. Dating, after all, precedes marriage; if you want to get married, you date. But dating is not supposed to be a way of life as it had become for this woman. Dating is intended to be the appetizer; marriage, the main course. This woman had overdosed on hors d'oeuvres—introductions, small talk, searching for something in common—and, for her the words "dating" and "abuse" became synonymous.

But no incredulous comments or sarcastic remarks came from the women who have experienced the realities of an abusive dating relationship. These were the women who told me their stories: the innumerable tales of date rape, beatings, degradations and pain. These private nightmares, shared here for the first time, are what compelled me to write this book.

I first recognized dating abuse in 1981 while speaking at a high school in the suburbs of Milwaukee, Wisconsin. As the director of a shelter for battered women, I often spoke to community groups regarding the issue of abused women and their children. At the time, I was one of the few staff who actually enjoyed talking with high school students about family violence because I wanted to give teenage young women an understanding of what could happen to them in the future. And, if they came from homes where violence was prevalent, I wanted to support them for what they'd already seen their mothers experience.

So I shared stories of women who left home with their children and came into the shelter in order to escape violence at home. I showed a film about a shelter and shared my concerns about what could happen to them later in their lives.

When I asked for their input, these high school juniors and seniors talked more about themselves and the guys they dated than they did about their mothers.

"Once when I was drunk and said something, he slapped me," said a 17-year-old. But because she was drunk, she thought that her boyfriend was justified in hitting her.

An 18-year-old dated a guy for four months before he pushed, slapped and hit her with a closed fist. She said that the violence was sparked by disagreements over drinking and drugs.

And a 16-year-old, who said her boyfriend hit her "too many times to count," was pushed, slapped and hit nearly a dozen times with his fist. She said that jealousy and anger over sexual denial ignited the abuse. Yet another teenager, slapped by her boyfriend when he was jealous, was asked if she thought he hit her because he loved her. She replied, "Yes."

Concerned about what these teenagers were telling me and with the hunch that these things weren't happening only in this one suburban school district, I devised a survey for students to fill out. Whenever I or someone on the shelter staff spoke in high schools, we asked the students to complete it.

Two things crystallized when I looked at the survey data from over 200 respondents.

First, dating abuse occurred at an alarming rate among high school teenagers in affluent suburbs. Over thirty percent of the young women surveyed indicated that they had already encountered physical abuse in a dating relationship.

Second, dating abuse was often seen as an "act of love." Of

12

those abused, one-third said that they were hit because their boyfriends cared for and loved them.

From this data I knew that two issues contributed to the magnitude of the problem:

- the alarming amount of physical and sexual abuse among teens and
- the misguided attitudes about acceptable, even desirable, dating behavior.

When I started talking to my friends—women in their 30s and 40s—about what I learned from these teenagers, I soon recognized that I was myopic in my original recognition of the problem. Initially, I considered *teens* who were hit by their boyfriends to be dating-abuse survivors and *adult women* who were abused by their dating partners to be battered women. But as I talked with dating women in their late 20s, 30s, and 40s, I recognized that it's not age that's the dividing line, it's the relationship.

Dating is not the same as living with or being married to someone. It's a separate and unique experience. I asked a 42-year-old single friend to read a magazine article I had written about dating abuse. The article focused on dating abuse among high school and college age people. I identified warning signs and what survivors could do to get help. My friend's comment helped me see the magnitude of what I was uncovering.

"These are things *I* need to know," she said. "This is as important for me *right now* as it is for teenagers."

Recognizing that dating abuse transcends age, I solicited accounts of dating abuse from women of all ages and I ran several classified ads in *Ms. Magazine* early in 1986.

> **First- and third-person accounts** for book on dating abuse—physical, sexual, emotional, verbal—wanted from women of all ages. Send comments or write for anonymous questionnaire. Claudette McShane, Box . . .

While I'd been *talking* about writing a book on dating abuse for almost a year, it wasn't until this ad ran that I felt *obliged* to write it. After the first classified ad appeared in *Ms.*, it took only a few days to get requests for my questionnaire. And the responses, which can be found throughout this book, left no doubt in my mind that dating abuse is a woman's issue which potentially affects all women.

Today, the dating experience differs decidedly from just a generation ago and dramatically from two generations ago. Then a woman who wasn't married by her mid- or late-20s was considered an "old maid" and hence, not courtship bound. Now, with many women delaying marriage until their late 20s or 30s, the dating years are no longer synonymous with teenage years. And the high divorce rate also means that women of all ages are reentering the dating arena—often with the same unsureness they had as teenagers. Hence, a 30- or 40-year-old woman can be just as vulnerable as a 16-year-old.

As with the businessman who puzzled over the relation between abuse and dating, others not affected by date abuse may question its existence. But those who've experienced its trauma have proof that it exists. Their physical and emotional scars are the constant reminder of their private nightmare. However, even they will be surprised at the extent of the problem and the similarities between their own and others' experiences.

With this book, dating abuse survivors will finally be able to name what happened. They'll be supported as their scars heal and as they learn what others have done to overcome the trauma. Their nightmares need no longer be private.

There's little doubt from the survivors interviewed for this book that dating abuse constitutes a problem separate from what is commonly referred to as "family violence." Some survivors sought help from battered women's groups but remained unaided. Others were told by the police that there was nothing to be done since this wasn't a domestic matter.

Yet, my experiences in working with battered women show me that there is a definite connection and interrelation between dating abuse and family violence. Since dating and courtship precede marriage, dating abuse could be considered the prelude to wife abuse. For many women, the abuse which began while dating continues and intensifies with marriage.

Dating abuse could be the most accurate indicator of future wife abuse and merits special attention to prevent dating-abuse survivors from becoming battered women.

The research conducted for this book was not intended to

produce hard data. On the contrary, after reading the dozen or so studies completed prior to the start of my research, I was convinced of the extent of the problem, at least at colleges where that research had taken place.

My purpose in conducting research, however, was twofold:
- first, to substantiate the extent of dating abuse among women of all ages; and
- second, to gain a wider recognitionof the problem by sharing experiences through the eyes of dating-abuse survivors.

Hence, the results can be labeled as "soft research" laden with personal accounts and observations.

This is not an apology but a recognition of the process I chose to use. For this book to be useful to its readers, I purposefully avoided heavy treatises comparing various research studies. My analyses of the numerous issues surrounding dating abuse stem more from a synthesis of the material and interviews I conducted than from empirical research of the field.

Because of this, something will surely strike a resonant chord in the reader. I say this from personal experience and the impact I've felt from the women I've spoken with. Initially, I referred to these women as *victims*. But later, I reframed my thinking and chose instead to call them *survivors*. This is not to minimize the fact that they have been victimized, but rather to put the labeling where it belongs—*with the act*—and not with the person.

When you read this book and if it relates to your own experiences, don't reject yourself and fall into self-blaming traps. No judgments are placed on these women and their stories, but often, ways of *understanding* what happened are revealed. Use what is helpful to you now and put the rest on hold for later if it is too difficult to sort through. While this book is meant to educate and support women, it may generate pain, anger and conflict. If this happens to you, don't go through this process alone. Find a friend, therapist or support group to help you through your feelings. Read the chapters on healing and prevention as a way to regain your power and control.

An understanding of dating abuse comes from sharing and talking with others, from giving this social problem a name, from offering help to survivors, and from suggestions to abusers and to communities on how to stop it. This book is a first step in that direction.

The women I interviewed share a common goal: to help prevent dating abuse. None of them had ever heard of the term when they were being abused; some of them didn't recognize that they had been in an abusive relationship until they were away from it. All of them want the problem out in the open.

Because I believe that little is gained in skirting the issue, the vignettes which are to follow in the succeeding chapters are just as the women told me and some include foul language and graphic details. You are sure to find some of it disturbing; and while I regret your discomfort, I hope that you will understand the survivors' pain and the need to share this information with others.

Part One

The Issue

1

They Always Promised Me a Rose Garden

Dating. When I asked a group of women to describe what their expectations of dating were prior to ever having gone out on a date, I garnered the following responses:

"Excitement."

"Romantic times."

"Perfect. Everything perfect."

"Chance encounters."

"Eyes locked across a crowded room."

"Sun-drenched beaches, elegant dinners, moonlit dancing."

"Prince Charming."

The "Dating Game"

It begins early. Before a girl is old enough to consider dating, she's already been enmeshed with multimedia portrayals of primping, prancing and romancing. Magazines from the pre-pubescent on up to the "older" woman of 25 to 40 are hard pressed to pass up an article on weight control, beauty tips or fashion. The often subliminal message clearly speaks to one thing: finding—and keeping—the man of your dreams.

With television, there is the more potent transmission of daily doses of the benefits of certain foods, diet plans, toiletries and exercise regimes. Sensuality, built into the most inane commercial ads, enraptures the viewer. We can become more beautiful if only we change toothpaste, soft drinks, or car makes and models. And a mere breakfast cereal can give us total nutrition and a slimmer body while we dreamily look into the eyes of our beloved. While we know on a cognitive level that these claims are ludicrous, they've been designed to capture us in our hearts with promises of love and romance. We may or may not buy the product, but we "buy" the message: *Anything For Love.*

Liquor commercials and cigarette ads play into the same theme. Have you ever noticed how many glass-toting and cigarette-puffing men have a woman at their side, or worse, at their feet? And it's all so attractively packaged that we imagine, *Me too! I can have that!* without recognizing that we've been duped once again.

And so the bombardment continues. Films, music, videos, novels and soap operas draw millions into their world of fantasy. We are enamored with lovers. More than 50 million single Americans, one of three adults ages 20 to 55 are potentially looking for love. But of course, in order to be a lover, one must first date. Therefore, a date—hopefully a long succession of dates with the same person—becomes a goal in itself.

While most women prefer to meet dates through friends, when that resource is depleted, women who want to date—so they can eventually fall in love and live out the American romantic dream—must resort to other means. Often this includes going to social gatherings, bars or singles functions. But when tired of these meeting places, many women turn to dating services or the classifieds—the matchmakers of the 1980's.

For the first time, women have an opportunity through these classifieds to initiate a romance from the safety of their own homes. The following ads are authentic. They ran in a midwest singles magazine in 1987.

> Close your eyes and imagine sharing winter with a special friend. One with intelligence, warmth and a gentle demeanor. One who believes that a relationship is

20

based on friendship, trust, mutual interests, understanding, sharing, affection and love. One who enjoys art fairs, escape weekends, creativity and laughter. This professional, attractive single white female, 35 years old, at 5 feet 8 inches, is adventuresome and fun-loving.

* * * * *

I'm yours—if you are a sensitive, creative, athletic, professional man, 30 to 40 years old with a good sense of humor who is seeking an adorable, professional intelligent, and funny woman, 30 years old, 5 feet, 3 inches tall, 120 pounds. I enjoy small luxuries but value the basics, love the city and the country and my spare time activities include movies, music and running. If you think that there might be chemistry, please send a letter, photo and phone number.

* * * * *

Anachronistic country gal adrift in an alien hi-tech world, seeks fellow traveler to share odyssey toward a simpler, stable, uncluttered, often silent, secluded, sensuous life. Divorced white female, 40s, tall, titian-haired, slender, non-smoking professional seeks rugged, ursine outdoorsman, independent thinker, reserved, emotionally discriminating, for home-centered pleasures, mutually constructed peace. Quiet, confident, ripe for discovery with literate lover, a wilderness-savvy "John Muir" type. How does one advertise for chemistry? If fundamental constructs are similar, details can be hammered out with time and tenderness. Have we cut our feet on life's same stones? Send photo.

At 60 cents a word, this last ad cost nearly $40 to run one time. For $40 this woman may receive several, dozens or hundreds of replies. It's up to her to decide which ones she'll respond to. And the magazine keeps her identity a secret. If she finds that special someone, then her money's been well spent. If no one shines above the rest, then she's out $40 and a lot of time spent culling through what amounts to junk mail.

These ads, and most of the others —several hundred in one month's classifieds—are anything but humble. For some women, this is an opportunity to say all those things they'd never have the nerve to say during a first encounter—in essence, *I'm a pretty terrific person*. Most of the women who place ads don't limit their descriptions to physical features, although nearly all of them make mention of height, weight and approximate age.

One of the biggest problems with such impersonal dating searches as classified ads and dating services is that most of the ads and the majority of the listings are placed by women, and most of the women are age 30-plus. This reinforces the much publicized shortage of available men and, as with any commodity in a capitalistic system, supply and demand increases the value of what is in short supply.

Women, therefore, tend to put an even greater emphasis on finding a man at the same time that men recognize they've increased their worth. In short, women, many of whom feel desperate to have a date, often settle for less. And they often drift into visions of the societal fantasies which have shrouded dating for decades.

A society in love with romance

So enraptured has our society become with dating and falling in love, we fail to recognize that much of what is portrayed in the media often depicts force, violence and humiliation under a facade of pleasure. Have you ever searched for an erotic movie in which both men and women are treated with decency and respect? It's a rare breed. Instead, the X-rated shelves abound with male pornographic fantasies.

We are a society in love with romance. But it's basically still men's notion of romance which is forced upon us and we, as a society, fail to recognize what this does to keep women vulnerable in relationships. While women consider a man's overall looks and are attracted to a certain "type" of man—such as rugged, scholarly, athletic—men care less about the whole and concentrate on body parts. Hence we still hear from the "breast man," the "leg man," and the "ass man." Men continue to insist that women primp but not appear "too done up." (Sound consistent with many make-up commercials?) And clearly men don't want women who are "too fat." (It's not surprising that most people with eating disorders are women!)

Because society promotes the notion of Prince Charming who will sweep women off their feet and take them into the land of lovers, women enter dating relationships on the premise that, if they can live up to society's idea of beauty, hide their flaws and have this man fall in love with them, all will be right with their world.

It's no small wonder then that when I asked women what their image of dating is now that they've dated, their responses took on an entirely different tone.

"It's a joke—a bad joke."

"A necessary evil."

"I'm afraid to date anymore."

"It's painful."

"Dating scares me."

"It's humiliating."

Yet, for all its pain and degradations, there continues to be that hope that the one true love—the one we as little girls dreamed about—will come into our lives. And because that dream lives, we support myths about dating which keep us vulnerable—and unequal—in relationships.

Prince Charming, where are you?

2

Fantasies and Fallacies:
Turning Myth into Reality

Myth 1: When you fall in love, nothing else matters.

We've all known someone who's forgotten about everyone else in her life because she's dating. Actually, if we're perfectly honest with ourselves, we've probably fallen prey to this practice at some point in our own lives. And why shouldn't we? We've grown up in a society which values dating, falling in love and romance.

After sitting around home every Saturday night or worse—going out looking for someone to date every weekend, you're entiled to drop everyone else in your life to date this kind soul, right? Well, you may think so, but I doubt if your friends do.

One of the problems with this is it puts far too much value on the date and the relationship. And as you continue reading this book, you'll recognize that this is a big reason why many women remain in abusive relationships.

Dropping out of your usual social circles, cutting time from your really long-standing friends, and playing into the nothing-else-matters game leaves you with just that—nothing else. Giving any man, or person, your total time, energy and attention puts him in a mighty powerful position. You're less likely to see the failures in the relationship, more likely to put up with abuse, and definitely are on the road to an unhealthy dependency.

When you fall in love, *you* matter, *he* matters, and the *rest of your life* matters.

Myth 2: Love means never having to say you're sorry.

We have Eric Segal to thank for this one. As the author of *Love Story*, Segal tells us that love precludes the need to say that we're sorry.

I've yet to observe a healthy relationship that didn't require a regular dose of *I'm Sorry's*. The ability to apologize, to admit fault and to recognize mistakes constitutes one of the greatest traits in a solid partnership.

Imagine that
- you accidentally stepped on your partner's toe with your hiking boots; or,
- you arrive 30 minutes late for a date; or,
- you unintentionally say something about him in front of his coworkers and see him grimace.

No need to say you're sorry?

On the contrary, if you don't say you're sorry, you're in for the building of a tall list of accumulative annoyances. Those are the little things that people let pass because they're not big enough to address at the moment or because someone doesn't want to extend an apology. The problem is, when not addressed and dealt with, they don't go away. Instead, they accumulate in a side pocket of one's emotions. When the last little thing occurs that the recess can accommodate, all rip out in one giant surge.

Then you'll hear about it—often all at the same time because the pocket rips opens and out it pours. Instead, a sincere *I'm sorry* could have dissolved the accumulating annoyance and prevented it from going into storage in the first place.

And when we look at the bigger hurts, the ones that explode all on their own the minute they occur, how can we excuse ourselves from apologizing?

Imagine that
- you decide to go out with his best friend without telling him and he hears about it from another source;
- you forget to pick him up from the airport as promised and he's stranded for hours;
- you talk about his birthday for months, then tell him you're not available to celebrate it with him.

If you aren't going to apologize for these things, it appears you don't really care about this relationship. Being in love means you're committed to say "I'm Sorry."

Myth 3: If he spends a lot of money, I have to sleep with him.

Too many women still feel obligated to the men who take them to an expensive restaurant, the theater, a concert or somewhere else where a lot of money's been spent on them. As the tab runs up, the woman's sense of duty rises. Admittedly, few women have had the nerve to pull away from a simple embrace or a kiss on the cheek from a date who has spent a bundle.

So what happens when he presses for more? It takes a strongminded—and sometimes strongbodied—woman to thwart the guy's advances.

One woman in her late 20s went to dinner with an out-of-town man who was the friend of one of her coworkers. After dinner and drinks at the expensive hotel where he was staying, she agreed to go to his room for a nightcap. When he started making sexual advances—pushing her back on the bed and telling her to take her clothes off—she adamantly refused. And while he attempted to pressure her by saying, "You know, that wasn't a hamburger I bought you tonight!" she refused to be coerced. Yes, he spent a lot of money on her. But she had learned over the years that she wasn't for sale.

So if he spends a lot of money on you, say *Thank You.* And if you want to be real bold, do what a cartoonist suggested—ask him if he wants a receipt!

Myth 4: He wouldn't get so jealous if he didn't really love me.

Jealousy and love are two of those feelings that intertwine in unsuspected ways. Most of us feel jealous when our partner appears to flirt with someone we consider attractive. It's what we *do* with the jealousy and how *real* the threat is that separates it from destructive acts.

When a man uses jealousy as a weapon in a relationship, often he blames it on his love for the woman.

- "If I didn't love you so much, I wouldn't get so jealous."
- "I can't bear the thought that someone else would want you."
- "I couldn't live without you."

What's left unsaid is that he's unsure of himself, insecure of his own feelings and mistrustful. Certainly we all don't want to lose our true loves, yet we generally don't dwell on the subject incessantly and look for daily reasons to be jealous.

One woman I spoke with told of her boyfriend's accusations whenever she went to her college classes. Because she dressed in coordinated casual clothes, wore an appropriate amount of make-up, and took time to blow-dry her hair, he suggested that she was dressing up to impress someone—male, of course. There was little regard for her need to look good for herself, much less the fact that she was a nursing student and her day was spent almost exclusively with other women.

In contrast, another woman who viewed little jealousy in her relationship commented that her partner, upon seeing her primped for a meeting, delighted with how terrific she looked.

If he really loves you, he won't try to control you through jealousy.

Myth 5: Dating someone is better than dating no one.

A woman told me about a close woman friend who for a time

would never agree to go out with her on a Friday or Saturday night. As her friend put it, "In case someone asks me out."

They both knew that the "someone" she was referring to was a man. And while this typifies teenagers' behavior even today, these friends were in their 30s, both professional women, and both with feminist leanings. Eventually, the woman who reserved weekend nights for unknown male suitors realized that she was cutting herself off from her true friends and spending needless time alone or with boring men. She no longer reserves weekends for those "just in case" dates.

There's another problem with dating just "someone." Think about the women you've known who've dated men who were real losers. Or, better yet, think about the losers you've dated. Why didn't we know at the time that they were losers? Or did we know—but were afraid to admit it because we were so desperate for a date?

One woman wrote that she thinks we date men solely because the men *ask* us to go out. It's not because we have anything in common. It's not because we particularly like the guy or even find him attractive. And it's not necessarily a man we'd sit around waiting to be asked out by. It's just because dating someone seems to be better than dating no one.

There are some single women who for periods of time decide that they'd rather not date. During these times, they don't go looking for dates; they don't sit home waiting for dates; and they don't spend time hoping and dreaming of dates. Instead, they refocus their energies onto themselves, their friends, their interests, their jobs. And they usually resurface from these periods with a more solid notion of who they are and, therefore, what they're looking for in a love relationship. Because they've survived or thrived during a dateless period, there's also the recognition that they don't have to settle for less.

They know that they don't have to date someone to be someone.

Myth 6: You're nobody 'till somebody loves you.

Okay, so Frank Sinatra had a point. We all need the love of

someone. But that doesn't mean that we have to take it to the extremes of looking for love from just *anyone*.

Do we need someone to love us? Yes. And it begins with *ourselves*. We need to delve inside before we can look outside for love. When we focus our existence as being tied up with someone else's love, we lose sight of the most precious and important person in our lives. Ourselves.

I'm not promoting isolation, self-adulation and narcissism, although I do believe that each of these can be had in healthy doses. In order to be receivers of love, we need to love ourselves. In order to choose healthy love relationships over unhealthy love relationships, we need to feel good about and *love* ourselves.

A recurring theme among many of the women I interviewed for this book is that they felt undeserving of real love and, conversely, deserving of the abuse they received from their dates. Why? Often it stemmed from childhood.

As the child of an alcoholic, a victim of incest, a battered or emotionally neglected child, we seek to fill the voids of our earlier childhoods. Our parents let us down and failed to teach us the early lessons of trust, autonomy, initiative, identity and intimacy. While we search for someone to fill our void, we usually aren't aware of these issues. We just know that we need someone to love us—and our childhood experiences have taught us that love often hurts.

Learning that we are somebody—somebody important and deserving of healthy love—is a major step in breaking out of the unproductive trappings of a lost childhood. When we love ourselves we're somebody.

Myth 7: You always hurt the one you love.

You need to wear a pretty thick shell not to be hurt by the one who loves you. An unkind word spoken in anger, a misunderstanding, a forgotten commitment, or any number of things hurt in relationships. Many of these are unintentional, unavoidable and forgivable after a little remorse on the part of the offender.

Unfortunately, many people expect that the hurts in a relationship will be deeper and more painful. They expect malicious acts or physical abuse. In a survey of 3,000 teenagers nationwide, one-third of the boys and one-fourth of the girls said that they expected husbands to hit their wives.

And while many women still believe that you always hurt the one you love, the ones who refute it may continue to have trouble when their dates still believe that love and pain are bedfellows. Many women who contacted me reported that their dates made remarks during sex like, "I know you like it rough." and "It's supposed to hurt the woman." When some women cried out in pain during intercourse, their dates didn't stop; instead they were often more turned on.

A solid healthy relationship can never be sustained with pain and hurt as an element. Instead, it must be supported by the mutual theme, "You *never* hurt the one you love."

Myth 8: He wouldn't hit me if he didn't love me.

When one-third of the high school girls I spoke with indicated that their boyfriends hit them because they loved them, I realized that this myth continues to flourish even today. Perpetuated by films, music and the media, women continue to be depicted as victims. A recent jewelry ad in a Chicago-area publication portrayed a man with a boxing glove at a woman's neck while her neatly manicured hand displayed an expensive and elaborate diamond ring. The caption read, "ANOTHER KNOCKOUT!"

Men also perpetuate this myth when they attempt to apologize or excuse their behavior with, "It's because I love you that I get so mad!" or "If I didn't love you so much, I wouldn't get so crazy."

And if we believe him and the myth, we forgive because as women we've been taught to be forgiving. When he appears remorseful, sobs or shows signs of regret, it serves to reinforce his love for us. For many women however, this is just the beginning of what will become an ongoing abusive relationship and possibly an abusive marriage.

As women, we need to believe a different script and to teach it to our daughters and our sons, "He won't hit you if he really loves you."

Myth 9: Men are innately superior to women.

Although many men support this myth, women fall prey to it also. Ever had a friend whose discussions centered on the current man in her life? Her good days/bad days depend on him. What he does, the food he likes, his hobbies, his plans, all consume her. She's always trying to fit herself into his life and willing to drop her interests—and often her friends—for his. And when the current relationship sours, she picks up the same pattern in her next relationship.

This is someone who believes than men are innately superior to women. And this is someone who's putting herself in a vulnerable position.

Conversely, a woman who believes in equality between men and women and trusts that her interests, job, hobbies, talents and friends are just as important as her date's is more likely to maintain an equal balance with her partner. If her newfound partner doesn't care to attend classical music concerts, she continues to go—alone or with another friend. She maintains her other interests, not out of spite but out of respect for their mutual differences. And if the man can't handle it, then so be it.

For this woman, her belief that women and men deserve equal respect takes precedence. An equal relationship has no tolerance for abuse.

Myth 10: Resisting a date's advances only enrages him.

Because the fear of rape is something we live with as women and because we often blame ourselves when we get raped, this myth serves to keep men in power and women vulnerable.

Although resistance can lead to anger, it doesn't always. And the anger doesn't always lead to rape.

When a woman operates under the myth that she can't resist sexual advances, she becomes prey to whatever man she's with. A woman who believes that she has the right to refuse sexual contact, the right to choose whom she will have sex with, and the right to decide when she will have sex retains more control over her destiny.

Some men will not rape a woman if she resists his advances. He's just living out the American male fantasy of taking advantage of a woman and getting her to "give in and put out." For some men, a clear and firm *No* stops the advances.

This is not to infer that a woman who's been raped brought it on herself by not stopping it. A man who rapes women may do so if she refuses his advances or not. And each woman determines for herself her need to protect herself in a life-threatening situation. Deciding to give in so as not to enrage a rapist may be a valid behavior.

But the decision to resist a date's advances is also valid. Men need to hear *No* for what it means and women need to stop being afraid to say it.

Myth 11: The Feminist Movement is the reason why men and women don't get along anymore.

This implies that before the Feminist Movement men and women did get along; i.e., men weren't angry with women and didn't abuse women.

On the contrary, before the Feminist Movement of the 1960's men abused women. The difference between then and now is that *now* women talk about it, protest it and take men to court. Now we have written laws punishing husbands for beating their wives. Before, unwritten laws condoned the abuse of women and, in earlier centuries, laws actually permitted the beating of wives by their husbands.

Those who choose to blame the Feminist Movement for the so-called "battle of the sexes" are angry with the dethroning of male power in relationships. Those in the Feminist Movement expose crimes against women; they don't create these crimes, and they don't promote these crimes. The Movement also opened the doors so that women can leave their homes if they choose and pursue stimulating careers in all fields. It has promoted and it supports equality for both women and men.

If a man claims that the Feminist Movement ruined male-female relationships, he either has a poor grasp of what those relationships were like, or he fears the power women really have. Because men tend to see relationships as *someone up/someone down*; they think that if they relinquish their superior position, they will become inferior. Women, on the other hand, have an easier time accepting the notion of equality and a shared partnership. Perhaps with time and experience, both men and women will recognize that the Feminist Movement has provided the foundation for male/female relationships to be built on mutual honesty and respect.

Myth 12: He needs me.

This is also known as *I can change him*. Socialized as women are to believing that we can transform all that is wrong in a relationship, we often fool ourselves into thinking that we will change our beloved.

If he drinks too much, knocks us around, gambles, uses drugs—whatever it is—we'll "get him to stop." And because we believe that we can do it, we reinforce the premise that "He needs *me* to become a better person."

This makes it particularly difficult to pull out of the relationship and give it an impartial review. Because of our role as *fixer*, we have a double investment in what happens.

Instead, we need to recognize that only those who help themselves will be transformed. An alcoholic needs treatment for his or her problem, just as an abuser, gambler or drug addict. And if you have a problem in needing to change him, then you need help for yourself. This help can be found at Alanon or other self-help groups and agencies.

For some women, the issue isn't as defined as "alcoholism" or "gambling." They just want to change some of his annoying behaviors:

- He often forgets to show up for a date.
- He puts you down in public.
- He pushes you around and sometimes hits you.
- He's rough sexually.

Does he need you in order to stop these behaviors? Can *you* change him?

No. But you can tell him what you think and what you feel. You can tell him what you need and expect. And if he respects you and cares about the relationship, he may decide to change.

But changing him is *his* job—not yours.

3

When the "Dating Game" Becomes the "Hating Game"

Defining "dating abuse" presents a challenge because it encompasses such a wide range of tolerances. What one person considers abusive may not be thought of as such by someone else.

One person may consider verbal abuse enough reason to break up with a dating partner; accusatory remarks, put downs or threats of violence may be intolerable.

For someone else it would have to be a slap or some other physical act before it constituted abuse.

Yet another person may not consider an act abusive unless it resulted in physical injury. A hit, push, shove, kick or punch which left no marks would be disregarded while the same behavior which resulted in bruises, black eyes or broken bones would not.

Personally, I have a low tolerance for abuse. I do not submit to put downs, snide remarks made in jest, teasing and, certainly, no forms of physical exertions of power. If I detect the slightest hint of abuse, I bring it into the open. I don't play *martyr* and I won't play *victim*.

Surely if I were to impose my abuse level on others, it would be ludicrous. It has taken me years to acknowledge it myself and it is based on my personal background including working in a shelter for battered women for six years. My abuse level is mine and mine alone. I can't give it to you; I can only explain it to you.

Definition of "Dating Abuse"

Dating abuse has been so readily disregarded in our society that it needs a definition which captures its subtle as well as its blatant aspects because I want the definition to apply to my low tolerance as well as to someone else's higher endurance of abuse.

With this in mind, my definition of dating abuse is

• *Any hurtful or unwanted physical, sexual, verbal or emotional act inflicted by a casual or intimate dating partner.*

To better understand, I'll describe the four categories of abuse.

Physical abuse

Physical abuse includes many forms of bodily contact including slaps, hits, punches, shoves, grabs, beatings, kicks, bites, chokes and/or use of a weapon. An abusive act does not have to leave bodily injuries to be considered physically abusive; it only has to be hurtful or unwanted.

- Are you frightened, intimidated or threatened by some thing your date did?
- Did a date ever shove you in anger?
- Do his fingers dig into your skin when he grabs you?
- Does your cheek burn where he just "playfully" slapped you in the face?
- Are there bruises from when he punched you in the arm?
- Is it emotionally difficult for you to talk about something your date did even though it happened a long time ago?

A *Yes* answer to any of these questions is an indication that physical abuse occurred.

Some forms of physical abuse are difficult to recognize.

Wrestling with a date, for example, in an agreeable, playful manner isn't abusive. But if it begins to get rough and you get hurt, it's gone from a *wanted* to an *unwanted* act and from *playfulness* to *abuse*.

A mistake on his part? Maybe. But if you tell him to stop and he won't, it's become abusive. The hurt from this wrestling match could be physical, as in a twisted arm or bruised leg, or could be emotional because by not stopping when you told him to, he's put you in an inferior position and used his power and strength against you.

For some, it's difficult to view an incident such as this as abusive because it began in play and was not done out of anger. But, it's abusive because it became hurtful and unwanted. What's critical here is that he didn't stop when you asked him to.

If you're stepping on someone's toe in a grocery store and the person points this out to you, do you ignore what was said and continue to step on his foot? Of course not. Instead you pick up your foot and apologize. Why should a date treat you with any less respect?

Our society accepts what's considered to be "non-aggressive" violence within the context of relationships. The classic "slap-in-the-face-to-calm-a-woman-down" has been seen for decades in the movies. For many, this is not considered an act of aggression but rather as a "therapeutic tool." If you observe young couples together, you'll see a lot of "playful" punches on the arm, slaps to the back of the head, pinching and arm twisting. And while it appears playful, many people—especially women—are hurt during this type of interaction. And it can lead to other more serious abuse.

While some forms of "playful" physical abuse are not readily identified as such, other actions blatantly constitute abuse. Little doubt exists around the labeling of such acts as beating, kicking, choking and using a weapon against someone.

Physical abuse might leave no physical injury, but it's more likely to minimally result in bruises. And it may result in serious and permanent injuries: loss of hearing from a hit to the side of the head; broken ribs from being kicked down the steps; kidney failure after a beating to the torso; vision impairment from a slug in the eye. And, yes, women are sometimes killed by their dating partners. Nearly one-fourth of women homicide victims are killed by their boyfriends or husbands.

Because of this life-threatening nature of physical abuse, no aspect of dating abuse should be taken lightly.

Sexual abuse

Sexual contact becomes abusive when it is unwanted. It doesn't matter that there may have been consenting sexual behavior prior to the abuse. Difficult for some to accept, prior willing participation in sex does not lead to an automatic consent on later occasions. And this is why so many victims of date rape fail to prosecute. Often they themselves don't fully believe that they were assaulted and, without that belief, they cannot proceed to convince others.

As with physical abuse, sexual abuse has a wide range of behaviors which may be hurtful or unwanted: an unwanted embrace, kiss or touch is on one end of the spectrum while forced oral, anal or vaginal intercourse is on the other. When sexual contact crosses over into hurtful or unwanted acts, it is abuse.

Sexual abuse can occur as a result of coercion, force, threats, trickery or pressure. To check this out one needs to ask

- Do I want to be with him, involved in sexual behavior right now?
- Am I doing this because *I* want to or just because *he* wants to?
- Do I want my date to be treating me this way?
- Am I in pain?
- Am I frightened or intimidated by my date?

As women we've learned society's lesson of taking care of men, not hurting their feelings, and giving in when we don't want to. Often we don't want to do something, but we don't know how to go about making sure it won't happen. We play into not wanting to hurt those "frail male egos," or we're intimidated by the strength and force our date has over us. Whatever the reason, often we succumb to sexual abuse.

Date rape, one of the most serious forms of sexual dating abuse, has only recently been brought to the public's attention. It is not, however, a new phenomenon. As early as 1957, a study in the *American Journal of Sociology* reported that almost two-thirds of the women surveyed on one college campus had experienced offensive sexual intimacy.

While social differences regarding sexually offensive behavior

38

in the 1950's and 1980's must be taken into account, nearly a third of the women in the 1957 study responded that they were subject to "attempted intercourse or attempted intercourse with violence." Undoubtedly the phrase referred to more than an "unwanted embrace" even three decades ago.

More recent data from the 1980's indicates that one-fourth of women in college experienced attempted rape or are rape victims. And, ninety percent of the victims know their assailant.

But, while date-rape statistics indicate that a woman is more likely to be a victim between the ages of 15 and 24, my surveys and interviews reveal that girls as young as 13 and women in their late 20s, 30s, and 40s are just as vulnerable to date rape.

Verbal abuse

Verbal abuse in a dating relationship often involves put downs, swearing, demeaning comments and threats.
- "You're a lousy cunt. No one else would want you."
- "Fucking bitch. Get over here!"
- "I don't know why I waste my time with you."
- "Who was that guy I saw you talking to?"
- "Why weren't you home when I phoned?"

Often verbal abuse ensues when a man feels emotionally or intellectually threatened by a woman who appears sure of herself. This is what happened to a 35-year-old social worker I interviewed. She dated a man several times before deciding that they just weren't a good match. On their third date, at her apartment, she told him that she didn't think they should go out anymore because they didn't have enough in common. He went into an immediate tirade, berating her for her pompous attitude.

"Who the hell do you think you are?" he screamed. His diatribe lasted for nearly an hour, during which time the woman didn't dare speak a word for fear that he would turn on her and physically abuse her. As a trained social worker, she knew how to counsel people and deal with their emotions. But this man's outrage immobilized her. When he finished, he stormed out the door and she's never seen nor heard from him again.

There probably are few people who haven't said a disparaging word to their partner in the heat of an argument. For some couples, though, verbal abuse predominates the relationship. When verbal abuse constitutes more than an occasional mistake and, instead, sets the tone of the relationship, it's an indication of the need to control the other partner.

Emotional abuse

Emotional abuse often occurs because of the continuing and deliberate *lack* of a behavior or response: giving a woman the silent treatment; ignoring her; pretending she doesn't exist; promising to do something and then not following through; withholding attention, affection or friendship.

Of the four types of dating abuse, emotional abuse is the most difficult to identify and quantify because it's more vague than other forms of abuse. The comments from women who filled out my questionnaire, however, indicate that emotional abuse can play a devastating role in dating relationships.

A 26-year-old woman wrote, "I once was dating a man who broke promises all the time yet made me think that we were really close. Then one day he told me he had leukemia and would be dead in a few months. He broke off the relationship and I never heard from him again. I mourned for him as I assumed he had died. Then, I saw him with another woman two years later."

This woman, left with her own speculations about what really happened, wondered what she did wrong or, more typically, what was wrong with her. Her sense of trust had been violated—both her trust in others and her trust in herself.

She may wonder, "Why didn't I pick up on his antics sooner?" "Why did he think that he could do this me?" "Why didn't I see through him?"

It's important to note that all of the cases described in this book involve emotional abuse. Sexual, physical and verbal abuse leave emotional pain for each woman, and the emotional trauma constitutes some of the most damaging and long-standing pain for its survivors. It's as if the emotional pain chisels an indelible groove in their souls. Ridding themselves of this pain is often difficult— but possible.

40

Part Two

What Happens,
Who It Happens To and Why

4

Sexism Is a Social Disease

Social System of Sexism

Clearly, some of the abuses in dating relationships, particularly those cited in the chapter on sadism, are manifestations of misogyny—the hatred of women. Misogynist men hate all women and they display their disdain through the abuse of the women they date.

Yet, other men don't qualify as misogynists. They don't hate all women. They don't deliberately try to hurt women. Rather they are part of the *social system of sexism*. And as the dominant species, these men sometimes blatantly and other times subtlely abuse women in what is often considered "socially acceptable" ways.

In the past, many of these incidents would not have been considered abusive. They would be everyday scenarios of women and men relating with one another. But today, we must sort out the absurdities of some of these behavior patterns to break out of the familiarity and acceptance of these practices.

Some men will read these accounts and set on a course of self-improvement. They will see themselves reflected in these vignettes and will suffer either embarrassment or guilt. The effects of their acts were never fully explained to them before. Now that they know the pain they're causing, they'll put effort into stopping it.

But other men will refute the incidents as another attack from crazed women who have nothing better to do but cry "Abuse." These are the men to be careful of for they are more concerned with protecting their turf than with respecting women.

In order to address sexism and dating abuse, I must use generalities. And so, while I realize that not all women or all men believe or act a certain way, I will categorize behaviors and attitudes into male and female beliefs.

Men feel superior; women feel inadequate.

These deep inner feelings begin in childhood when parents dress baby boys for function and baby girls for show. For example, try someday to put on a dress and crawl around the floor or up the stairs. Feel inadequate? These female feelings continue with the promotion of boys into "real" sports like football and hockey, "real" subjects like math and science, and "real" jobs like engineering and science. And yes, while strides have certainly been made to balance the opportunities afforded to boys and girls, girls still suffer handicaps which impede them in the climb to success.

Men play out their superiority in dating relationships in a variety of ways. Clearly date rape is an act of superiority *plus* aggression. Any form of physical abuse asserts a man's dominance over a woman. But the subtleties of verbal and emotional abuse also demonstrate that women as a class are considered inferior to men.

A 24-year-old Kansas woman wrote, "The number of times he put me down and demeaned me in front of others is impossible to estimate. The relationship lasted three months and was pervaded by this negative attitude. He seemed to delight in making me feel like the most insignificant person in the world. He even made fun of me for having gone to college! He, needless to say, was woefully uneducated.

"An example of his cruelty: He calls me on a Friday night—"Hi babe, what're you doing tonight?"

"Oh, nothing, why?"

"Well, I'm going to this great party. I thought about taking you, but—nah."

Because men and women operate on different systems, women believe that relationships have the ability to be equal, so that neither partner has to be over or under the other person. Men, on the other hand, believe that in every relationship someone is superior and someone is inferior. Therefore, a man can't allow a woman to feel as though she may be adequate because he fears that he could lose control and she may dethrone him in his superior position. Some men have an incessant need to humiliate and embarrass the women they're with in order to maintain their supposed superior status.

Julie, a 23-year-old New Yorker, wrote, "A boyfriend of six months would volunteer to help me do my grocery shopping. He was very helpful, but, then every time we got to the car in the parking lot—with my arms full of grocery bags—he would, especially when people were walking close by, fake a serious, angry air and yell absurd things at me like, 'Matilda, you slut! Why did you sleep with those guys?' or 'Linda, you whore! No! I can't have sex so much. It makes my you-know-what hurt.'

"I would try to live through each unexpected episode, but it made me feel extremely embarrassed. I told him to stop it. And when I did my shopping alone, he would embarrass me at other times: in my own driveway, at the pharmacy, in the school halls, etc. He would always apologize afterwards but repeat the behavior at other times and locations."

The variety of ways in which men play out their superiority is endless. Some use verbal put downs and attempt to embarrass, discredit or shame their dates. Others prefer to intimidate their date through a show of force. Still others, like the man who'd explode absurdities in the parking lot, invent their own means for "keeping women in their place." One woman wrote that her date would often wake her by pouring no less than a quart of ice water on her head. Even though she pleaded with him to stop, he was amused with her distress and continued to entertain himself at her expense.

Women discuss why they want to end a relationship; men avoid it.

Many women told me of situations where they were dating a

man for months or years; then suddenly he dropped out of sight with no explanation or warning. There's such a commonality in the stories these women told me that it wreaks of social bias against women.

A 44-year-old Massachusetts woman wrote, "What happens to me, in fact it happened this week, is that a man I expect to hear from again never calls. This is usually without any advance warning whatever and even despite promises that if the relationship ended he would tell me or discuss it with me. The man that especially comes to mind was a minister and counselor. To me this behavior seems unethical. I would never think of doing this to a friend. Of my relationships over the past four years, every one has ended this way except the one that I ended; and when I ended it, I made a special effort to spend the time needed to discuss it with him, give him a chance to express anger, etc. And this was after much discussion of my problems with him and what I thought were constructive efforts to work something out. But men won't tell you that there's any problem. They just disappear, often after seemingly becoming closer and more intimate."

Another woman in her mid-40s expressed similar concerns. She'd been dating a man for several months. They'd seen one another a few times a week and talked as often on the phone. The man spoke of things they'd do together like trips they'd take over the summer months. Shortly before he ceased to call her, the woman initiated a discussion about her need not to be deserted should the relationship end. Clearly uncomfortable with the conversation, her date discounted it by saying that he had no intentions of breaking off the relationship and that there was so much they planned to do together. Yet, just a few weeks later, he stopped calling—totally disregarding her discussion with him on the need not to be deserted.

Perhaps men think they are being kind when they ignore women in this way. After all, it avoids a scene—tears, angry words, displays of hurt feelings. But in reality, what men avoid is sharing in the pain. For the pain is still there, but now it becomes the woman's alone to endure. There is no chance for closure, no words from him about what happened, no opportunity to work things out together.

Some women, tired of being discarded like a used-up tube of

toothpaste, try to find out what happened. Frustrated with being ignored, angry over being deserted, some women contact their former dates and ask them point blank, "What happened?" The replies are classic.

"One time I confronted a man about being stood up for a date and he acted as if it never happened.

"When I called to ask him why he never called me again for a date, he said it was because I didn't perform oral sex on him after he said he loved me."

For one woman, her partner informed her of their break off when he called her with this comment, "If you want a date this weekend, you'll have to find someone else because I already have one."

Sara, a 32-year-old New Yorker, told about a break-up of a recent relationship which she was involved in for about a year. "I finally believed this was it—I'm older and wiser so I was more willing to compromise," she said.

In April she found out by accident that he was engaged and had been for two years. After about a month, he claimed to have broken off the other relationship and Sara felt confident as they arranged a 4th of July vacation together. Since they weren't going out of town, their plans to do local things were flexible. For Sara, Independence Day was more than she had bargained for.

"Every day was a new excuse why he couldn't see me. On July 3rd he slept over and the next day he left, planning to meet me later that afternoon—No show. I got a call later that evening in which he apologized. Of course, foolish me accepted. He was coming over—Again, no show. The next morning I saw him—he works in my building—He was sorry. He would take me to dinner that night. But I had plans and, thank goodness, I kept them."

The following day while Sara was out, he called and left a message on her answering machine. He wouldn't be around because he was attending his wedding!

Sara said, "He talked a great story. Looking back, my relationship was filled with no-shows, extremely late-shows, apologies and unexplained hours away from me. I was so honest and trusting."

And on the whole women *are* more honest and trusting in relationships. Women trust that men will be this way also, but all too often it doesn't occur. Yet, as women, we enter the next relationship believing, and hoping, that it will be different this time.

Men prefer sex; women prefer affection.

When women are asked if they'd rather have sex or cuddling, most answer "cuddling." Men, on the other hand, prefer sex. But the real issue here is that the question should ever be posed. That there'd be sex without cuddling is like trying to bake a cake without turning on the oven.

Yet, sex without affection is the *modus operandi* for many men—particularly those who believe that men have a greater need for sex than women. For these men, sex is a necessity; affection is not. But for women, affection is the necessity and sex without it is abusive.

Many women report that their date's sexual attentions are rough and fast. Though legally not "rape" since the woman consents to having sex, nevertheless, this type of behavior is a form of moral rape: using another person in a way which is painful and at times destructive.

The following scenario typifies this type of interaction.

"It was during my junior year in college that I was dating the man who would commit a near rape. I say 'near' because, while I had agreed to sexual intercourse, he consummated the act in a rough and brutal way. We had been seeing each other for several months. After one of our dates, he asked if he could spend the night with me. I agreed.

"When we got to my room, he undressed quickly and fumbled at my clothes so vigorously that I thought he was going to tear them right off. He kissed and sucked my neck and breasts so hard that the bruises remained for several days afterward, and my nipples and areola were tender and swollen. He penetrated me quickly, with little preamble, and thrust himself in deeply.

"Though I wasn't a virgin, it was quite painful, especially since his penis was so long and thick that I would have required careful arousal to be able to receive him comfortably. After he withdrew, my labia were swollen and sore. When I got up to urinate, it hurt to walk and the pee burned as it touched raw tissue."

And if all of this wasn't enough abuse, this man added another

48

insult when afterwards he asked her, "Do you want me to put it in again?"

Some men are so out of touch with reality that they don't recognize when a woman is in pain. Their ideas of sex concern themselves, their own pleasure, and nothing more. That a man would honestly believe that a woman would enjoy this type of rough and inconsiderate treatment is a testament to the acceptance of pornography as the state-of-the-art in sexual behavior.

So many women wrote of incidents which portray typical pornographic scenes: rough man/passive woman; satisfied man/abused woman; man in control/woman in submission; man commits rape (legally or morally)/woman is confused and often blames self.

Because society reinforces these behaviors through movies, magazines, music and the media, both men and women have difficulty breaking out of these sexually abusive behaviors. And when women refuse to accept a man's notion of sex over her own need to have affection with sex, she's often seen as castrating, frigid and uppity. Or, she's approached more aggressively to be "taught a lesson."

Women also feel betrayed when men try to exploit a woman's need for affection. Several women reported incidents similar to this woman from Maine.

"Here's a line I've fallen for several times: 'We don't have to do anything you don't want to. We'll just cuddle a little, then sleep. Please stay, it's been so long since I slept with a woman.'"

The honorable intentions, however, dissolve with the twilight as he presses for sex. She continued, "I've given up several male friends after falling for that one. There's no worse feeling than being duped by someone you had cared about."

Women want to be treated as individuals; men want women to play out stereotypes.

So full of impact is the media image of women as sexy, thin, slinky and demure that many men insist that the women they date fit this mold. The pressures, both subtle and blatant, reinforce the notion that there is only one way to be a woman. And that way is the way men—collectively and individually—say it will be.

From a 21-year-old Wisconsin woman, "Many times I had dates who emphasized that I should dress sexy, be ten pounds thinner, wear corsets, high heels, etc. Similar things have happened to friends of mine."

Another woman reported that her boyfriend told her that if she loved him, she'd agree to anal sex, shave off her pubic hair, and be photographed nude by him. And although she was opposed to all three things, she reluctantly complied.

Often the pressure of our culture's expectation that women are sex objects to be used by men overshadows all else in the relationship. A college student from New York wrote of a scenario in which she unknowingly participated.

"A guy whom I adored and whom I considered to be my best friend kept inviting me to visit him at his fraternity house. We'd go into his room and talk, laugh and have the most cheery times together. He said that he loved me. Often, as I was leaving, he would go to the shower after bidding me farewell. I never thought much about it. Well, two years later, I was quite horrified to learn that my friend's showers were a signal to all his fraternity brothers that he had had sex with me! The real truth, however, was that we *never* had sex together."

This woman also recognized why her friend often wanted her to scratch his back—so hard—before she left. "I figured out that he wanted those scratches on his back as physical evidence for his frat buddies to prove that he had 'conquered' me."

There are also the stereotypes about emotions: women have too much and men shouldn't have any. One woman wrote about the first man she dated in college. "He prided himself on being very aloof and detached. So, he didn't want to hear about my problems and concerns. My mother was divorcing my physically abusive father at the time. My date also didn't believe in showing any physical affection in public. He wanted me to act 'like a lady' at all times—as opposed to a human being."

Another stereotype some men still believe is that if a man spends money on a woman, she'll sleep with him. Numerous women recounted incidents where men pressured them into having sex by saying such things as, "I spent time and good money on you. Now, you owe me sex."

Fortunately more women have gained the confidence to veto sex and are refusing to be "bought." When one woman refused to have sex, her date got nasty. She said, "He told me that's what's wrong with women. They take men's cash and won't give up pussy."

And yet another stereotype which still haunts women is that they're tainted and cheap if they engage in sex.

A New York woman in her 30s wrote, "I have been in two, long-term, serious and very sexual relationships in which I gave all my heart and soul—thinking it was being returned. The end result was both these men left me to marry virgins. They did not want their wife to be an experienced sexual partner." She added in her defense, "I have not been promiscuous—these were so-called 'relationships!'"

A 20-year-old Pennsylvania woman had a similar experience. "This guy begged and pleaded with me to sleep with him. Then he called me a whore and a tramp when I finally gave in."

And a California woman suffered the same sort of accusations. She wrote that when she became pregnant in her early 20s, she decided to tell her boyfriend since he had promised her that if it ever happened they would marry. She said, "After telling him that I was pregnant, he became so angry that he beat me badly and said it wasn't his baby and then for weeks he wouldn't even talk to me or touch me. He'd call me a 'tramp' and a 'whore' in front of other people and then when I was eight months pregnant, he said he couldn't take being around me because I had someone else's child and again he beat me. I delivered a son who died ten days later."

Sexism. It is a deadly, destructive weapon used to keep women inferior and men in control. It's a social disease against which both men and women need to be inoculated.

5

It Can Happen to Anyone . . .

. . . except me, you may be saying if you're someone who's been fortunate to avoid dating abuse. In reality, however, none of us are immune. We could all find ourselves, today or tomorrow, in a dating-abuse situation.

In fifty percent of relationships

One thing is for certain—dating abuse is so widespread that someone you know has already been abused in a dating situation, perhaps a friend, coworker or relative, someone who is 13 years old, 22 years old, or 45 years old. She may not have told you the details, but if you know what to look for, you'll be able to recognize her hidden pain.

If you're a woman who's dating right now, there's a fifty-fifty chance you'll suffer some sort of abuse by a dating partner. If you're not dating now, it's probably because you're married or living with someone, you're in a religious order or you're in some sort of a self-imposed moratorium on love.

Whatever the specifics of your non-dating lifestyle, one thing holds true: none of the above guarantees you permanent security for life. One of two marriages fail; even marriages to God aren't immune to failure; and love moratoriums can be temporary condi-

52

tions. So if you're not dating now, you very well could be dating sometime in the future. And that will put you in that fifty-fifty category for potential abuse.

An equal opportunity social problem

If you're still not convinced that dating abuse could be your problem, consider the following. Dating abuse presents itself in every corner of our society. It can happen to teenagers or older women; to uneducated or college-degreed women; to blue collar workers or professionals; to city residents or country dwellers; to white women or women of color. Dating abuse can occur on the night a woman meets her date or after months, even years, of dating. It happens in casual and intimate relationships; in straight and gay relationships. Like wife abuse, dating abuse knows no prejudices of race, geographics, or socio-economic status. For women, it's an equal opportunity social problem.

When I began working with battered women in 1976, I didn't know that my friends or acquaintances had been abused. Once I recognized the immensity of the problem, I realized that I did know women who were abused.

A relative told me of her live-in boyfriend and how he had once choked her into unconsciousness when she tried to break up with him. Afraid that he would someday kill her if she tried to leave again, she agreed to marry him. Yes, she was a battered woman.

A volunteer who worked at the shelter came in to work one hot summer day in a long sleeve shirt and oversized sunglasses. Sitting down next to me, she rolled up her sleeve to reveal her bruises and took off her sunglasses to show me the black eyes her husband had given her the night before. Yes, she was a battered woman.

I remembered from my past the family whose dad would come home drunk and break up all the furniture. Neighbors talked of the screaming and the wife and kids fleeing the house. We observed fear in the children's eyes; the pain and bruises on the wife's face; the cycle of picking up the pieces and starting again; the hope that this was the last time. Yes, she was a battered woman.

In fact, it became commonplace even at social occasions to have someone tell me about themselves or someone they knew who'd been abused. In a short while, I went from believing in fragments of the Ozzie-and-Harriet-Homelife-Dream to wondering if there were any truly peaceful homes. The years taught me that reality lies somewhere in between.

Dating abuse surrounds us in similar ways. Recognizing the signs, both in your own relationships and in what others are telling you, will help you to comprehend the immensity of the problem.

Reading this book may jar your memory—and emotions—in unexpected ways. After giving a talk to a social work class at a midwest university, one of the students came up to speak with me. Asking me to call her for an interview, she said, "I didn't recognize I was raped until I heard you talk. I never told anyone what happened, but now I want to tell you." For years she had kept this "secret" inside of her, not knowing what she was harboring and not knowing how to name it. Hearing me explain dating abuse and what other women had gone through gave her a framework to explain what had happened to her. She had been date raped.

Similarly, other women wrote to me telling me that they never told anyone about the abuses they suffered—sometimes because they were so young; sometimes because they were scared; sometimes they feared what their parents would say; other times they didn't think anyone would believe them; sometimes they didn't know what to call it; oftentimes they thought they were to blame.

Now that women are speaking up and are sharing their stories, they've named it—dating abuse. And it can happen to any woman.

But, because all people have the capability of hurting others, men can also be victims of dating abuse. Size and physical strength, however, generally give men the edge in any physical or sexual struggle. And while there are some abused men, most men who are physically abused by their partners are abused in reciprocal acts of violence where both the man and woman injure each other.

Although a woman may hit her date, much of the violence is in retaliation to the man's abuse towards her. Often, it's in self-defense. Usually it's only the man who perpetrates more serious acts such as choking, threatening with a weapon or rape. In short, it's the woman's life not the man's which is seriously endangered.

This is not to minimize any serious injuries men may suffer; it is only to put it in perspective and to explain why this book deals with dating abuse against women.

Abuse in lesbian relationships

Gay relationships must also be recognized as having dating-abuse survivors—physical, sexual, verbal and emotional. Although not the focus of my survey, some gay men wrote that they are involved in abusive relationships.

About ten percent of the women who contacted me reported such abuses in lesbian relationships.

Do cases of abuse in lesbian dating relationships mean that dating abuse is not a form of violence by men against women? No. The underlying issue in dating abuse is not the gender of the abuser; it's the perceived attitude and power of the abuser. When one person considers himself or herself as more powerful or has a need to be more powerful, that person finds ways to control the other. Dating abuse is a manifestation of this need to control and, as such, can occur in any dating relationship regardless of sexual preference. It occurs primarily with men abusing women because of our social structure which for centuries has promoted male domination over women.

While dating abuse in lesbian relationships is addressed here, this book refers to the abuser as a male since most of the respondents to my questionnaire were women reporting cases of abuse by their male dates.

Dating abuse is a complex and widespread problem. While it can happen to anyone, there are ways to avoid much of it. But in order to gain control over what is controllable in dating abuse, we first must learn to recognize it in its many manifestations.

6

The "Dream Man" Becomes a Nightmare

Remember those images of Prince Charming sweeping us off our feet? Well, for some women, they met Prince Charming and he not only swept them off their feet—he knocked them halfway across the room!

Meeting Mr. Right isn't as simple, or as wonderful, as projected in the movies. It's especially discouraging if you've dated a lot and have gone out with more than your share of losers. So when you finally meet, or think you've met, that special person with whom you're in sync, it's a dream come true.

For the women whose stories are shared here, their "Dream Man" turned into a nightmare. The man that seemed to be so sensitive, so caring and so wonderful turned on them. Just when they thought they had all they ever wanted in a man, their bubble was burst by the very person who bought them the balloon. And this is what makes their pain so difficult to bear.

When the perfect date turns on you.

One young woman, Tricia, met her dream man in high school. They had known each other for three years prior to going out. After dating for three months, Rick asked Tricia to go to the senior prom with him.

Tricia remembered, "We were going to be the best couple. He encouraged me in finding a formal dress and constantly raved about what a great time we'd have."

Then, just one week before the prom, without warning, he ignored her totally.

"He avoided me in between classes. He stopped calling me and didn't answer my calls," she said. Tricia didn't go to the senior prom. "A $100 dollar dress . . . unused. He took his ex-girlfriend instead."

A few weeks later, Tricia called Rick and asked him why he stood her up. "He said that he didn't like the color of the dress I bought and that I wasn't good enough to spend the evening with." But, she continued, "I learned two weeks later that his ex-girlfriend promised to sleep with him and he knew I wouldn't."

Perhaps Tricia was young and naive. Perhaps she had built up her expectations of Rick. Perhaps. But it doesn't minimize the affect this breach of promise has had on her. Since this time, she's been in a series of abusive relationships, most with the same pattern of meeting someone she adores then getting deceived by him. She's searching for someone to trust but can't seem to find him. For Tricia, and other women with a similar pattern in relationships, building an ordinary man into a "Dream Man" becomes a setup for abuse. Had Rick treated Tricia special, taken her to the prom as he had promised, and followed through on his talk of having a great time, Tricia's expectations for a relationship might be different today. She may have learned to trust—herself and the guy she is dating.

For another woman, Cheryl, she met the man she thought was to be her "Dream Man" after many years of dating. Never married, at age 35, Cheryl had a series of positive dating experiences. An interior designer by profession, one summer weekend she visited a woman friend in Chicago's prestigious Lake Point Tower.

Her friend had gone to see a client so Cheryl went to the outdoor pool on the premises. She said, "I met a nice looking, divorced, well-to-do man who also lived in Lake Point Tower. He was in the advertising field. He had green eyes like I do and the same color hair, so I somehow took to him right away and trusted him. I guess my guard was down."

In a soft spoken, almost mystical voice she continued, "From the pool he suggested that we go up to the top of The Tower and have a drink. So we went up there, but the bar was closed. It didn't occur to me at the moment but now I think that since he lived there, he would have known the hours in which the bar was open," she said in retrospect.

"So, he asked me to come to his apartment, and he'd make us a drink while I gave him some interior design suggestions."

Having taken an interest in her profession and with the trust and connection she already felt for him, Cheryl agreed.

"He made something for me to eat, we had a nice talk, and I gave him some design suggestions. Then, all of a sudden—pow— and I'm on the floor." She remembered her shock at his actions.

"He started making sexual advances, and when I resisted, he began to bang my head against the floor. I knew that if he kept that up, I'd be unconscious shortly. So I decided to cooperate," she said.

"Then—he actually thought I was enjoying it. When we were sitting on the couch with his arm around me, afterward, he even asked me if I liked it. He clearly had a weird perception of what went on."

One of the things which surprised Cheryl the most is that they both were obviously attracted to one another and had he been the kind, gentle person she thought him to be, she would have willingly had sex with him if he had made appropriate overtures.

"He was such an attractive man, he obviously didn't have to be violent with women," she said. "I thought we both had an interest in each other." Unfortunately, his intentions turned in a direction Cheryl never imagined.

Before the assault, Cheryl had said that she was to catch a train later that day back to her hometown. He had offered to drive the one-and-a-half-hours to Cheryl's home and at the time, she accepted.

After the assault, he was still talking about taking her back. Obviously, by this time Cheryl had changed her mind. "But I had to figure how to get out of his apartment because he had bolted the door. I knew that if I tried to open the door, I might not succeed and might be hurt again."

Instead, she told him that since she wouldn't be on the train, she'd have to call a friend to tell her not to pick her up.

"He said, 'Sure. Go make a call,' pointing to his phone. I told him that the number was at my friend's apartment in my suitcase. He said, 'Then dial Information.'"

Thinking quickly so she wouldn't appear to be frightened, she told him that the number was unlisted. He believed her.

"So, he let me out. And did I run. I got into my friend's apartment. But I didn't even have a chance to lock the door and he was right there."

Luckily Cheryl's friend had come back, and then Cheryl made it very clear that she was not going home with him. He finally left.

While there were no lasting physical damages from the sexual assault, Cheryl had a headache for the next couple of hours. But she expressed something that few women say. She claimed, in her very quiet way, that this experience didn't have a negative impact on her. Since she had dated a lot of men prior to this assault and had all positive experiences, she put this in the perspective of one incident out of many. The man also did not live in her hometown and did not have a way to recontact her. But, she said that while she didn't attempt to prosecute when this occurred (it was twenty years ago), she definitely would if it happened today.

Perhaps Cheryl's assault was less traumatic to her because she didn't have a history—longer than an afternoon—with this man. As a successful professional woman who owned and operated her interior design business, Cheryl's life didn't crumble when the assault occurred. Instead, she saw it as a bad experience, didn't blame herself and went back to her hometown without fear of seeing this man again.

And yet, for all of the internal strength and self-esteem that Cheryl seemed to have when I interviewed her, she asked if I could help her understand why today she is 55 years old and has never married. She wonders if there is something about *her*, if she scares men off, if she should act differently.

For another woman, Paula, her "Dream Man" was more than an afternoon's acquaintance. At age 25, she was engaged to Jim. Only after the engagement did Paula recognize that Jim was someone different than the man she hoped to marry.

As with many abusive men, Jim slowly controlled Paula's life and her social contacts. By the time she broke up with him, he had excluded her from "attending bridal showers, baby showers, or even visiting my sister. So one time when I planned to attend a close friend's baby shower, he toyed with my spark plugs so the car sputtered and spat; then he sat home waiting for me to come running to him to fix it."

Trying to work out the problems between them, Paula suggested that she and Jim go away for the weekend to a cozy cabin in northern Wisconsin.

"Saturday, we had a nice time biking, enjoying the fall colors, hiking, etc. I was exhausted after dinner so while he watched TV, I fell asleep. He was extremely upset that we did not get 'close' that night.

"In the morning, he was cold, distant, then argumentative. I wanted to go home but he insisted on taking a ferry with our bikes to a nearby island," she remembered.

After arguing the entire 45-minute ride on the ferry, Paula and Jim biked in separate directions.

"He found me twenty minutes later, pushed me off my bike and started to yell while he hit and punched me. I screamed as loud as I could and scared him off," she wrote.

Later, after the car ride back to their hometown, Paula told Jim that she never wanted to see him again.

"He couldn't understand. He proceeded to threaten that some day he will get even with me, so that when I am least expecting it, *something* will happen," Paula continued.

"This loving, gentle 'Dream Man' that I was going to marry turned out to be the most deceitful, evil man I ever knew. I am still living in fear even though five years have passed."

Were there clues that Paula could have picked up on sooner? Often there are in situations like this. In Paula's case, I don't know if there were any clues since she filled out her questionnaire anonymously and I have no way of contacting her to ask.

This next woman, Brenda, was given a clue. However, it was a clue that she regrets was only recognized in hindsight. She wished she had heeded the warning and hopes that other women learn from her near fatal mistake.

Four years ago, Brenda, who lived in a small eastern town, met the man of her dreams. Brenda's boss introduced her to Daryl, a tax accountant, and that first evening they went to dinner with her boss and his wife. Brenda considered Daryl to be the perfect gentleman, the man every woman longs to meet. He was attentive, fun to be with, had lots of style, wore an expensive suit, gold watch and chain, and drove an expensive foreign car. Besides, he was her boss's friend, so she felt as though she knew him—and trusted him—instantly.

Daryl stayed with Brenda's boss that week. Brenda remembered that they went out every night and quickly developed a close and romantic relationship.

"When Daryl returned home to Baltimore, I received flowers and cards almost every day," she said. Never before had she been treated so special. Brenda knew her dream man had arrived.

Unexpectedly, Brenda was offered an excellent job in Baltimore. She was delighted to accept and found an apartment close to Daryl's. They spent a lot of time together enjoying concerts and extravagant dinners. Brenda, at peace with herself and with Daryl, enrolled in an MBA program at a local college.

Then one day, Brenda answered her phone and was unexpectedly speaking to Daryl's former girlfriend who was calling to tell Brenda that Daryl had a violent temper and that she had better watch out for him. But Brenda, sensing the resentment of a lost love, dismissed the warning. It was a warning that should have been heeded.

"Oh, if I had that time to go over; if only I had listened," Brenda reflected.

The first sign of Daryl's temper came a short time later when Brenda bought the store brand of cola instead of Coke. Daryl was so incensed that he threw Brenda into the wall. She had bruises not only on her face but down one side of her body. Daryl cried afterwards and said he'd never do it again.

"And, of course, I believed him," says Brenda who wasn't willing to turn her back on her "Dream Man."

But that was just the first of many times she was thrown into the wall, dragged from her car by her waist-length hair, and used as a punching bag. It's hard for Brenda to fathom now, but she was convinced by Daryl when he said it was all her fault and that she was the reason he did this to her.

"The horrible thing was that I began to believe him and I would apologize for making him do these things to me," she said.

Then one night, while Brenda was studying at Daryl's apartment, he brought home a purebred cocker spaniel which he began using like a punching bag and throwing it against the wall. Alarmed at how he might hurt the dog, Brenda abruptly stopped studying, grabbed the dog and held it to prevent further harm. Before Daryl could respond, a friend of his came over and after a couple of beers, Daryl gave the dog away to his friend. Brenda was relieved that the puppy would no longer be harmed but had no idea what was now in store for her.

After his friend left with the dog, Daryl came over to the table where Brenda was studying and began cursing at her, blaming her for having to give away the dog. Brenda started to respond, then decided against it. She didn't want to make the situation any worse than it already was.

But Daryl needed no argument from Brenda. He grabbed her by her hair and held her down. Then he proceeded to pick up a heavy wooden chair and crack it over her back. While she tried to fight him, it did little good; Daryl's strength and size outmatched her.

"Again I ended up against the wall. I felt so dizzy but I tried to pick up my books and purse and head for the door. He had gone to the bedroom and I figured I could sneak out," she said.

Brenda was wrong. Daryl caught hold of her hair going out the door and this time pulled out a chunk from the roots. He dragged her into the bedroom and threw her on the bed hitting her head on the wall again.

When he started to kiss her, Brenda thought that it was over—until he began to bite her right through her clothes. Even now, four years later, she has a scar where he bit her on her breast that evening.

"Then he pulled out the gun . . . and I knew it was loaded," Brenda remembered. She told Daryl that she was leaving and he responded by saying that if he couldn't have her, no one could.

"He put the gun to my temple so hard that I had a lump there afterward," Brenda said.

Brenda started talking to him, telling him that she was going to call his mother who'd be so ashamed of him. Brenda asked that he give her the gun before they both got hurt.

"Finally, after what seemed an eternity, he gave the gun to me.

He then started crying hysterically and lay on the floor, asking me to hold him. He said he was so sorry, he would never do it again. I knew that if I got out of this one, I would never give him the chance to."

Saying that she would get him a glass of water, Brenda left Daryl sobbing while she took the gun, threw it in the trashcan and left the apartment. She was afraid that he would follow her but he didn't. Her scalp was bleeding, her eye was black, blood was coming through her blouse where he bit her, her face and cheeks were bruised and she had numerous cuts and scratches on her face and arms from his fingernails.

It took Brenda years to overcome her pain. She tried for help first from the police but help was denied because they weren't married. She stayed home from work for a week, curled up in her bed, never dressing. Then she called a battered women's shelter and talked with a counselor on the telephone, but she didn't feel any better although she now recognizes that this was her first step in getting help.

Brenda heard from Daryl a few times after that night. Each time he came to her apartment, drunk and armed, she called the police. Again, the police were less than protective.

Within a year, Daryl left the area. Four years later Brenda said that she is engaged "to a very sensitive man, one who knows about this incident and is so very kind and loving." Knowing how close she came to death, she is thankful to be a survivor.

What happened to these women could happen—and has happened—to any of us. These women didn't build up these men unrealistically. Instead, they met men who appeared to be kind, honest and caring. They laughed, had good times, and opened themselves to falling in love. They trusted that what they saw, heard and felt was genuine.

Should they have been more cautious? Should they have been suspicious?

Only Brenda had a clue—the phone call from the former girlfriend. But she, like many others in love with a "Dream Man," had no other information to put that phone call in the proper perspective. Had there been other warning signs before the phone call, she may have sensed the danger she was in.

But Brenda, like most of us, believed that we can trust those we know and that we know those we trust. When this trust is violated, we often don't recognize that it's happening. If Daryl had been a loser from the start, Brenda may never have tolerated any of his abuse. But he wasn't a loser; he was the epitome of a "Dream Man"—and the "Dream Man" became a nightmare.

7

Under the Influence

Making excuses for men who drink

When blending alcohol or drugs with abusive behavior, the responsibility for that abusive behavior must lay with the person who is abusive. This is a critical point; too often, women claim that if only he hadn't been drinking or if only he wasn't on drugs, then he wouldn't have hurt them. The alcohol or drugs become an excuse. By blaming the substance, women excuse men for their abuse towards them.

A 26-year-old Illinois woman wrote, "Two of my dates shoved or pushed me. One man did it twice. He was taking some local marijuana and came to my apartment and shoved his way in. Apparently, he had a strange reaction to the drug. He pushed me several times toward the bedroom and then onto the bed. Then he raped me."

Her statement that he apparently had a strange reaction to the drug undermines the fact that he raped her. Perhaps he did have a strange reaction. But that in no way excuses or minimizes his behavior. He is still one hundred percent responsible for his actions; he raped her as much as someone who wasn't under the influence of drugs.

While it cannot be denied that alcohol and drugs may alter

one's behavior, once we begin to lay the blame with the *substance,* we take it from the *person*. And let's face it, "not guilty by reason of intoxication" is not a valid defense.

A woman in her early 20s wrote, "I dated a guy and once when we were together he had been drinking and he would not leave me alone. He was real rough about sex. He would not let me go and was hurting me—forcing me—to have more sex."

This woman didn't fall into the trap of excusing her date's behavior. She didn't pretend that everything would be fine if she didn't see him while he was drinking. Instead she connected the behavior—both the drinking and sexual abuse—with him. She said, "I never saw him following the incident. He kept asking me out, but I never dated him again."

Alcohol and drugs can also be used against women in another way. A midwest woman in her mid-20s felt coerced and tricked into sexual contact through the use of what she called "potent alcohol and drugs."

"After being given these substances by her date," she said, "a date arranged—unbeknownst to me—to have two male friends join a sexual encounter. They continued to perform sexual acts upon me without my consent."

"Taking advantage" of a woman under the influence

Numerous women wrote of situations in which they were out with dates, had been drinking, and then either passed out or were physically unable to stop sexual advances. The dates apparently sexually abused them, but most of the women remember little of the details of what transpired. They do know, however, how they felt afterwards.

After passing out from drinking too much, a 20-year-old Pennsylvania woman said, "I was bruised and sore for several days." She knew she had been assaulted, she just didn't know the details of the assault.

And a 19-year-old New York woman wrote, "I must have passed out from drinking so much. When I woke up, we were at his parents' house. I went into the bathroom and noticed that I had a huge hickey covering my entire neck, bruises on my body, and my underpants were stained because he must have pulled my tampon out."

Sexually abusing a woman who has drunk too much or taken too many drugs apparently is a more common behavior than we care to realize. I'll never forget how shocked I felt while talking to a man I went to graduate school with. Wanting to know his personal beliefs on the topic of rape, I asked if he knew anyone who had raped a woman. He casually told me how one woman he had dated drank too much on one of their dates and he had sexual intercourse with her after she had passed out. His rationale was that they would have had sex if she had been coherent so, as far as he was concerned, she'd given her consent. He felt no remorse. And this was a man who was getting a master's degree in social work!

While this type of male behavior isn't unknown, it's often not spoken about as routinely as it should. There are some parents who warn their daughters about drinking too much and being "taken advantage of." But do they really explain what that means and what to do if it happens? And are there parents who similarly talk to their sons about treating girls with respect and not "taking advantage" of them?

One woman equated drinking with abuse so seriously she won't even go out with someone who drinks. This Tacoma, Washington, woman wrote, "I almost got raped when I was 24 years old. But I got out of the car and got away. I have avoided men who drink ever since." Although this constitutes a way for this woman to feel safe, she must realize that drinking—or drugs—do not cause men to rape, and that men who are not under the influence of drugs or alcohol also sexually assault women.

Drug dependency

Ongoing relationships also occur in which one or both partners have an alcohol or drug dependency. Both partners may be chemically dependent; or one may be dependent and the other co-dependent. In either situation, the alcohol or drugs control the environment and the relationship.

A 30-year-old Wisconsin woman wrote, "My boyfriend worked as a bartender and I was unemployed. One night I met him at work and stayed until he got off. We were both pretty drunk and got into some petty argument—I can't even remember what it was about.

"At some point he started saying that I was helpless and worthless, and that I couldn't do anything to get out of my unemployed situation even if I wanted to.

"That night, I attempted suicide with tranquilizers because I believed what he said."

This woman makes other references to drinking throughout her survey, and I can only surmise that she herself has a drinking problem. Her dependency on her boyfriend, both emotionally and financially, plus her dependency on alcohol probably contributed to her attempted suicide.

A New York woman in her early 30s said, "I am dating someone who is a coke addict. He constantly blames me for his slips, puts me down in front of others, punches me and then acts as if nothing has happened. Many times I'm afraid to speak to him because I don't know what kind of mood he'll be in."

An Atlanta, Georgia, woman wrote about a man she dated when in her early 20s. "I was dating a man approximately ten years older than myself who, though I didn't know it at the time, had both an alcohol and a mental problem. For no reason whatsoever, he would often go into a rage and verbally put me down and tell me that I was worthless, etc.

"It took me a few years after the fact to realize that the tirades were probably really aimed at himself. I think his self-esteem was non-existent, and he wanted to take mine away from me as well. He didn't succeed."

Yet for another woman, her boyfriend's drug dependency led to a weekend of horror. It occurred "with a man whom I really loved and once had hopes of marrying." For this 30-year-old Texas woman, her nightmare lasted the entire weekend. She recalled this as a culmination of events whereby after each date she worried more about his potential for violence. And while she was in a relationship with a drug addict, it wasn't until the end of the relationship that she recognized it.

68

"In the months before this weekend, he had held very little respect for me. Sex was expected, which most of the time I didn't mind. However, on this last weekend I went out with him, I enjoyed nothing." Later she learned that he was using cocaine and she believed that this was causing many of his problems.

"One thing that had bothered me for a while was that he would not want me to remove my pantyhose and panties before sex. He wanted to rip them from me," she said.

"Okay, I should have stopped that, but I could sense what saying *No* would mean. He always paid me for the clothes, which he felt big about. I began to feel like a prostitute and was hoping to come to some understanding with him when he exploded," she said.

"The weekend he held me prisoner, he almost destroyed his apartment. He was unable to afford the cocaine that week and our date on Friday began the horror. That night he held a loaded gun on me and sodomized me," she remembered.

But the horror hadn't ended there. She wrote, "Claudette, on Saturday morning, three of his friends, one of which was his drug supplier, raped me and sodomized me repeatedly. I was made to give blow jobs over and over. All of this got him his cocaine for the week." And while she hadn't touched drugs prior to this weekend, they forced that on her too.

Not until Sunday morning was she able to escape. She said, "Very early Sunday morning, I left after he passed out on the floor. I was very hurt physically and mentally."

Clearly in this case, drugs were a motivator. Had her boyfriend not needed drugs, would he have done this? There's no way of knowing, but I would surmise that any person who could do this to someone he purportedly loved would be capable of doing it without drugs.

8

Barbarous Acts of Sadism

An alarming amount of sadism—the act of enjoying the infliction of cruelty as a sexual perversion—is reported in dating abuse. For me, these were the most difficult accounts to read. For the survivors, their pain—both during and after the incidents—was often insufferable.

Private pain/public lessons

I share these stories reluctantly. They are extremely personal narrations filled with intense cruelty. I've chosen to include them because the women who've suffered this pain wanted the accounts to help others. But in sharing them, I hope that these stories will not be used by voyeurs, to raise eyebrows or to cast dispersions on the women who've been victimized. Refrain from blaming the women for the atrocities that happened. And while you may want to question why one woman dated a guy in the first place, why she agreed to go somewhere, or do something, please look beyond her actions and realize what was done to her. Join me in affirming that no one has the right to treat anyone the way these women were treated. For some of you, as for me, reading these incidents may bring about feelings of anger, sadness, hopelessness and revenge.

Sometimes I cried, swore or sat quietly immobilized.

I shared the events with my husband when I knew that what I'd read or the interview I'd just done could affect my own relationship. I did so not as a voyeur or a pitier, but as a way for him to know that I needed special kindness because I, as a woman, felt vulnerable.

After reading or talking to women about these sadistic accounts, I always felt supported for writing this book. I knew that it was a way to change these private memories into public lessons. And I believe that for the survivors, sharing these stories gave them a therapeutic tool to aid them in working through their long-standing grief.

Many women wrote of painful intercourse and being forced into performing sexual acts against their will. For some, they suffered silently, not able or willing to tell their abusers that it hurt. They held back out of embarrassment, shame or fear of being hurt more.

Yet for others—some who told their dates that it hurt—it resulted in increased pain.

"Once when we were having sex, he asked if he could have anal intercourse with me," said a 25-year-old Indiana woman. "I said *No* but he proceeded to hold me down and do it anyway."

Why would this man ask, then not accept her answer? Certainly society's image of women as unwilling sexual partners plays a role in males' continuing this behavior. Scenarios portrayed in pornographic films and magazines are filled with male fantasies of sexual power and control over women.

This same woman went on to say, "Another man got very rough in bed and I expressed my discomfort. He held my arms, threw me on the floor and got considerably rougher. I had open sores on my hands and arms from the rug burns."

Sadism in dating relationships appears to be supported by a male subculture which promotes men's pleasure and women's pain. Many women report that if they indicate they're in pain, their date continues anyway. And often the man will support his beliefs by telling the woman, "I know you love it." or "You like it rough."

For these men, their misguided notions of sado-masochism have led to women's intense suffering and even fear of death.

71

Cruelty as sexual perversion

A 24-year-old Kansas woman wrote, "All of the biting, choking, hair-pulling and spanking took place within the context of sexual acts. I did not enjoy, encourage or consent to any of these basically sado-masochistic practices; my inexperience, fear and passivity were exploited.

"The most hurtful were two incidences of choking. I was totally powerless to stop them; the only thing that prevented him from actually choking me to death was his own last minute realization of how far he'd gone.

"It was always during intercourse that he liked to inflict pain on me. From his position on top, he could get his hands around my neck and gradually tighten them without my even being able to move away. As breathing became almost impossible, I would literally black-out and 'see stars.' I really don't know why he didn't ultimately kill me, except that when he finally reached orgasm, he lost interest in it!"

Although this woman protested his actions afterwards, it had little effect on him. On other occasions, this same man would force her to perform fellatio "by literally sitting on my face," she said. "Nearly suffocating me, he was totally oblivious to the tears running from my eyes, interpreting the sounds I made as moans of pleasure and forcing my head into his lap."

If this sounds like rape, it's because it is. It is sexual assault under the guise of what some men consider "normal sex." And because men so often control sex—and the relationship—women become entrapped in relationships which hurt them in many ways. Many women believe that all women are abused in relationships; so when their date abuses them, they do not have a perspective which allows them to see the horror of what they are enduring. They may date a man for months, or years, before they recognize the extent of the abuse.

A 19-year-old New York woman wrote, "I went out with a guy for a year and four months. We had sex everyday regardless of whether I wanted to or not or if I was in pain. One day, he forced his penis into my anus. I was in a lot of pain and screaming and crying. He just turned up the music and hit me everytime I tried to move out of that position."

Several women wrote of sadistic experiences in which their dates brought along other men and watched as the woman was repeatedly violated by his friends.

While obviously this is gang rape, what makes it even more painful is that it was arranged by a boyfriend. Someone trusted and cared for had set her up to be raped.

Another university student wrote from New Jersey. In her first year of college, she said, "While making love, my boyfriend would talk dirty to me. He would say things like, 'I'm gonna fuck the hell out of you!' Then he would get very excited and would thrust very hard inside of me. I would explain how I was in pain and he would reply 'It's supposed to hurt!' He wouldn't stop.

"He made comments like, 'Women need a good beating every once in a while. It'll keep them in shape.'" She continued, "Every time we made love, it was bad. I felt pain. He was often drunk, forceful, cold, stubborn and animal-like."

Most certainly not alone but feeling alone nonetheless, this woman who's just in the beginning stages of learning about love relationships had few past experiences to help her recognize the extent of her boyfriend's abusive attitude.

Because of this, young women—especially teenagers—are often extremely vulnerable. Of all of the accounts of dating abuse, the most sadistic and most painful for me to read came from a 28-year-old woman in Oklahoma.

Forced bestiality

She wrote, "When I was 16, I dated a guy who was 25. My parents didn't know it, and they would not have approved. He was divorced. After we saw each other a few times, over about two months, I let him take my top and bra off to play with my breasts, all of which I enjoyed. I was a virgin. After about two or three more months, one night we were together, and I got hot enough to want to give him my virginity.

"So, as he was playing with me, I undressed. I didn't tell him why. When he saw my tampon (I was on the first day of my period), he went wild with rage. He told me he didn't like menstruating women. Actually he said he wasn't sexually aroused by a woman on her period. I was scared, especially since I was horny and didn't understand his revulsion to my period. I didn't care that I was on it. I was horny and I wanted to give him my virginity.

"He calmed down a little, enough to tell me that his ex-wife insisted he perform oral sex on her during her periods, which he did for awhile.

"With a wild look in his eyes, he said to me, 'I know what you need.'

"Then he grabbed me and tied my arms to the bed with two belts. He returned with some rope and his Doberman. I began to think that he was going to beat me up or something. He used the rope to tie me, face down, spread eagle to the bed. He was so large I couldn't do anything anyway. He told me not to make a sound, and I never cried out, even once.

"When he began to put pillows under me, so as to raise my buttocks, I knew that he was going to give me to the dog. I was scared to death, but I didn't plead with him to stop, nor did I scream. I was thinking that I was being punished for seeing him behind my parents' back.

"He took the tampon out and let the dog smell it and lick it. It excited him immediately. I felt strange in the position I was in with my ass so high in the air and my legs spread. He led the dog onto the bed, and not more had I felt the touch of the dog's penis on my vaginal lips that I felt a searing pain. With that one hard thrust, the dog broke my hymen.

"He continued to fuck me for what seemed like hours, though I know it wasn't. When the dog was finished and out of me, this guy untied me and took me to the bathroom and told me to take a shower. I did, even though I could hardly stand up."

She said that afterwards he took her home and threatened that if she told anyone, she'd have to pay. She believed him, obviously, and while she never had any contact with him again, she'd see him in town from time to time. She didn't tell anyone. Not until she met and fell in love eight years later did she feel safe enough to tell her partner.

When she wrote to me, she said that I was only the second person she had shared this with. Her courage in writing down this painful, sadistic experience is why I decided to include it in this book. Choosing to remain anonymous, even with me, she said that she was, and is, "very embarrassed over having a dog take my virginity, especially since I know what it was—rape."

None of the women whose stories are included in this chapter reported their assaults to the police. On a very personal level, it isn't difficult to understand why. Would many of us have the courage, stamina and self-respect to endure the scrutiny which would accompany a report to authorities that our date—in most cases someone we'd been involved with sexually—had abused us through acts of sodomy, gang rape or bestiality?

9

"Crimes of Passion"

I was just trying to break up with him.

"I was just trying to break up with Jerry. He screamed, 'You'll never get away from me!' and started choking me. I tried to fight him off but I couldn't. There was a lot of yelling and because Jerry was in my dorm room, other people heard us. I went blank . . . I'm not sure how he let go of me. I think some people from the dorm came running in and pulled him off of me. When they took Jerry out, he was strapped down to a stretcher. That's what a maniac he had turned into."

Marilyn, nearly 30 years old and eight years out of this relationship, was visibly upset when she recalled the night her boyfriend almost killed her. It was the worst incident of many she suffered during the six years she and Jerry dated.

Jerry hit Marilyn over twenty times during their dating years which began while they were in high school. And she hit him as often. But Marilyn, at 5 feet 4 inches, 100 pounds, said that Jerry was a solid 6 feet, 200 pounds—hardly an equal match. Yet for Marilyn, it was important to her to try to fight back. "Every time he hit me, I hit him back. I wasn't just going to take it," she explained.

A lot of the violent incidents centered around what Marilyn considered unprovoked jealousy. "He used to accuse me of flirting with other guys all the time. There was no truth to it, but he wouldn't listen to me."

There were times when Jerry would taunt Marilyn. Once when they were on a deserted road outside of the city, "he stopped the car, pushed me out and drove away. I had no way of getting home and both of us knew it. There was no public transportation. He drove around the block, pulled up beside me and stopped the car. When I grabbed the door handle, he moved forward. He kept doing it until finally he let me in. He laughed and expected me to be grateful. It was humiliating."

After high school, Marilyn thought that she had a chance to get away from Jerry. She decided to go to college in another city while Jerry would remain in their hometown since he didn't plan to get a college degree. Marilyn was thrilled to get her acceptance to college, but instead of getting away from Jerry as she had hoped, Jerry had also applied and was accepted to the same school. They left their hometown together, Marilyn to live in a dormitory and Jerry in an apartment.

Shortly after starting college and while Jerry was visiting her in her dorm room, Marilyn decided to tell him that she wanted to date other guys. She carefully told Jerry that she thought that they both should date others because they had gone steady since they were sixteen. She knew that Jerry wouldn't be pleased with her suggestion, but she never expected that he would try to kill her. Marilyn realized that Jerry could have choked her to death that night if others had not intervened. After that, dorm authorities barred Jerry from coming to her room or even entering the building.

Marilyn's relationship with Jerry didn't end immediately after the choking incident although she remained firm in her desire not to see him. But eventually Jerry's harassments—on the telephone, waiting for her between classes—wore her down. He begged her forgiveness, said he was getting help, and pleaded with her daily to go out with him again. Feeling trapped, with no way to get him out of her life, she decided that if she dated him again at least he'd stop harassing her day and night. And even though Jerry never physically assaulted her again, the effects of his abuse towards her lingered. She had violent nightmares with Jerry appearing in her dreams trying to hurt her. And she was cautious in dating other men, fearing that she could be abused again. Eventually she made a clean break from Jerry and she moved to another state.

Four years after she and Jerry no longer saw or spoke with each other, Marilyn married Jim. While there's been no abuse in her marriage, Marilyn has had to slowly learn to trust that she won't be hurt emotionally or physically.

"When I first started dating Jim, I was afraid," Marilyn said. "Because we were getting closer, I'd get scared that I'd be hurt. Sometimes I'd have to leave. I'd get anxiety attacks."

Although Marilyn's experience left her with long-standing emotional scars, she's one of the lucky ones. For many women, "just trying to break up" results in death.

Murders and attempted murders

The media generally refers to these homicides as "crimes of passion." Unfortunately they're frequently sensationalized in a voyeuristic way. The accounts often take on a tabloid quality with references to heated arguments and lovers' quarrels. And while there is mourning for the victim, rarely is there social uproar over the extent of such murders.

In 1977, a 24-year-old woman was stabbed to death by the man she was breaking up with. Laura had dated John for about fifteen months.

In an article in *Mother Jones* magazine, Laura's sister Carolyn Weaver wrote, "It was hard to believe, even after it happened, that a woman—feminist by conviction, perceptive not naive—could lose her life because she had rejected a man."

Carolyn explained how, during John and Laura's relationship, there was a bossiness about John as he pressured Laura to marry him. He even told her that her refusals only confirmed that she was dominated by her parents. Eventually Laura tired of the relationship and decided that it needed to end. And like many women, she wanted to end the relationship without a scene. But John, not able to accept Laura's decision that the relationship was over, threatened suicide.

However, instead of killing himself, he went to Laura's home. She let him in and they stood and talked in the kitchen. It was nearly 1 a.m. and, not realizing that anyone was still up, Laura's father came down to the kitchen to shut off the light. When he saw John, he suggested that John go home and come back the next day to talk. Laura's father left the kitchen, and as he was getting into bed, he heard Laura scream. It took John less than a minute to stab Laura 15 times. The wounds were too numerous and deep to save her.

John was found guilty of murder and received a 25-year sentence. Eligible for parole only six years after Laura's death, if he isn't paroled and continues to be a model prisoner, he will be unconditionally freed in 1990, only 13 years after committing murder.

What is it about some men that makes them turn to violence and killing in the wake of a break-up in a relationship? John made a tape recording and brought it to Laura's house the night he murdered her. In it he said, "I now have an understanding of the worthlessness that I carried around with me and the ... distrust and anger and hatred that I generate ... " Did he expect Laura to fill his void, to make him worthy? Her refusal to continue the relationship was clearly the catalyst for destroying the veneer which kept him out of touch with his real self.

Similar issues surround another dating homicide. In May of 1987, Suzanne, a Wisconsin woman, was murdered by the man she was trying to break up with. Suzanne was 23 years old the night that Peter, age 35, shot her in the head then killed himself.

Unlike Laura, Suzanne had already severed the ties to Peter, a man she had dated in Colorado while she was in college. She had broken off the relationship five months earlier, but Peter persisted with phone calls and letters. Seeking to protect herself from his harassment, Suzanne moved back in with her parents in a middle class suburb.

Suzanne worked in a downtown shopping mall and the store's owners even notified security that she was being harassed by Peter. When she was leaving work one evening in May, Peter abducted her in the parking lot. A lot attendant witnessed the incident and notified police who contacted Suzanne's family. When police were told that Suzanne was being repeatedly harassed by her former boyfriend, they went to Peter's apartment. Only they were too late. Both Peter and Suzanne were dead.

Considered somewhat of a loner, Peter could not accept the fact that Suzanne didn't want to date him anymore. Suzanne wasn't trying to hurt Peter; she merely wanted him out of her life. She didn't want to fight with him; she just didn't want to see him anymore. The price she paid was death.

And, in yet another situation reported on television, three women disappeared on the west coast after dating the same man. In each case, the woman had been dating Robert for some time, then decided to break off the relationship. Each woman arranged to see Robert with the purpose of ending their romance. Each met him in a public place such as a restaurant, then was never heard from again. Yet, while this same thing happened to three women, there was not enough evidence to bring Robert to court. Another appalling factor in this case is that prior to the disappearance of these women, his former wife also disappeared—after asking for a divorce.

Once again, we are dealing with a man who seemingly believes that a woman's rejection of the relationship is a rejection of him as a person. Two commonalities exist in each of the cases detailed here.

- The woman took time to explain to her date that she wanted the relationship to end. And she did that because she didn't want the man to be unduly hurt.
- In turn, each man either attempted murder or killed the woman.

So what we are left with is a social anomaly:
woman as protector even as she is about to be murdered.

In another case of attempted murder, a 17-year-old midwestern woman was threatened with an ax and handcuffed to the rear bumper of her former boyfriend's car. Again the situation revolved around the break-up of the relationship which was initiated by the woman. Before this vicious act, the couple were to meet in a designated spot to return the rings they had given to one another. Instead, the guy grabbed his former girlfriend, forced her into his car while he drove. She was held in a headlock, and when she tried to get loose, he threatened her with death.

When the car stopped, he took her out of the car and sat her down on the ground. He stepped on her hand, then he dropped an ax just an inch from her fingers. He threatened to cut off her fingers.

He handcuffed her to the rear bumper of the car, but before that, he kissed her and told her it was the kiss of death. Then he forced

80

her to run behind the car or be dragged. Eventually he released her and drove off.

Often victims of murders and attempted murders involving dating partners are young women in their teens or 20s. But this is not always the situation. Many are women in their 30s or 40s. In one such case, the woman was 44 years old and the mother of four children. She and her husband had separated and she was romantically involved with another man. The man she was dating had entered into several violent disputes with the woman's estranged husband. Although the full details will never be known, the woman's new partner stabbed her and threw her partially nude body in the river. Then police found his body hanged in a cemetery with a note that he was involved in her murder. They had been seen earlier in the day arguing in front of a liquor store.

When we refer to these murders and attempted murders as "crimes of passion," we legitimize them in a way that demeans their victims. "Passion," a word which has cross meanings, can refer to sexual love as well as an outburst of anger. How absurd that our society allows these meanings to coexist in the same word. Were the victims murdered out of love or out of anger? The ambiguity serves to titillate the public when we allow the media to portray these acts of murder as "crimes of passion."

Hopefully we will begin to recognize that "crimes of passion" is a misnomer. That these are crimes, yes; but that it involves passion as love, no. Most of these crimes consist of cold-blooded murder. Often, the woman is first sexually assaulted, then killed. These are the facts which need to be highlighted. That there was a relationship—a sexual relationship—prior to the murder is relevant only to establish that the killer knew his victim and most likely premeditated the murder. It tells us about the murderer, not the victim.

10

Coercion:
Compliance under Duress

Possibly of all the scenarios involved in dating abuse, coercion is the one which leaves women the most confused.

Pressured into doing something which she doesn't want to do—but ultimately giving in, she finds it difficult to assert that she's been abused, even raped. Sometimes force or the threat of violence is involved. But often, the situation consists of more subtle coercion comprised of insistence, bullying, dominance and intimidation.

Subtle coercion

Sandra, an 18-year-old college student on the east coast, said, "The first time we did it (had sexual intercourse), I didn't want to. I only knew him one week and had no birth control. He called me a baby and said I was a little girl when I started to cry. He acted as if it was my obligation since I was his girlfriend—so I gave in."

And for Sandra there was another element—fear. She continued, "Plus I was scared of him. He was over six feet tall and in excellent shape from daily working out."

Besides the coercive belittling and fear, Sandra's boyfriend added a third element to further confuse her. She said, "He told me sex was supposed to hurt the girl."

Consequently, at such a young age and with few other positive experiences to tell herself that this wasn't right, she continued to date this guy. The result, she said, was that "every time we made love, I felt pain. He was often drunk, forceful, cold, stubborn and animal-like."

Later, this same guy used his coercive techniques to con her out of money—a scarce commodity for a college student. Finally, she realized that she had been lied to and deceived. "When I got conned, my whole life fell apart. My trust in anyone ceased."

For this woman, the subtleties and pressures around sex clouded her abilities to comprehend what was happening. But the taking of her money crystallized this man's demeanor for what it had been all along—deceitful and abusive.

Many women spoke of being belittled when they refused to have sex. The following scenario encapsulates what a lot of women have endured.

A 21-year-old college student said, "My date told me that I was immature sexually. He accused me of acting like a 13-year-old. He put me down and treated me like a little kid. At the time I felt bad about myself and ended up having sex with him to prove him wrong."

Later when she was away from him, she justifiably felt angry. Preying on a woman's vulnerabilities, be they related to age, physical appearance or emotions, gives the man an unfair advantage. It's another con game.

Other women told about having their vulnerabilities exploited by men whom they went to in order to get emotional support.

"When I saw an old friend of mine during a really bad time for me, we spent the evening talking about how I was being used by guys. It was wonderful—he listened, told me the guys were rotten and that I deserved better. When he put his arm around me, I leaned into him like I would to my big brother. This was a guy I had known for almost ten years during which time we never had a romantic relationship. You can imagine how shocked I was when his hug turned sexual. And yet, I was too vulnerable to resist his advances. All the while we were having sex, he made it seem like he was the only one worthy of me. Only much later did I recognize that I had been used again."

Although many women fall into coercion in an almost naive way, others—usually those who have been through it before—can spot it more quickly. A woman in her mid-20s, who is a banker in Georgia, is more in touch with subtle coercion.

"Basically, the only problems I have ever had sexually with a dating partner is when I am made to feel guilty about not pleasing him, and not necessarily wanting sex when he wants it, or in the position he may want at the time," she said.

"This especially happens after a disagreement when he wants to 'make up' and I want to talk." She asked, "Why is it that the majority of men feel that sex solves all problems?"

A chronic complaint of many women, men tend to use sex to make up while women need to make up before they can have sex. By not tuning into a woman's needs to be on solid footing before making love, men often set themselves up to be seen as uncaring and coercive.

Manipulation

And while sex may be used as a means to make up, some men also use it to manipulate the woman. Many women related situations in which they were told that if they didn't have sex, the relationship would be over. Or when sex didn't result naturally from the relationship, the men found ways to manipulate the situation to their advantage.

An Indiana woman wrote, "Men have told me that they loved me and made dates in the future and promised me the moon for a night in bed—after which I've never heard from them again."

This same woman said, "Another man got hysterical when I told him *No*. He cried and said he was homosexual because there were no women to teach him about 'normal' sex and he threatened to kill himself. I felt guilty and gave in—never to see him again."

A Wisconsin woman said, "I began having sex as a college student, but I didn't particularly like it. My boyfriend would always pressure me and sometimes almost beg. He would get kind of disgusted and I would sometimes give in just to shut him up, but it made me feel like one of those inflatable dolls. It took me a very long time to be able to enjoy sex and feel good about it."

Preying on a woman's guilt is a most common form of coercion. Many women told me of this type of persuasion. One woman from Pennsylvania remembered a guy she dated in high school.

Nancy said, "I dated a boy named Mark. I didn't like fooling around with him (I didn't realize until years later that I'm gay) but I did because I felt I should. He was very rough with me, I think without realizing that he was being rough. I always was very adamant about not going all the way, and the very thought of oral sex made me ill, but I finally gave in once on each count.

"He didn't threaten me; he just made me feel guilty, so that I did it to make him leave me alone. I felt very degraded both times. With the oral sex he really didn't give me a choice—he just shoved my head down and put his penis in my mouth. I felt dirty for days after that incident."

Dominance

It is not unusual for women to lose their virginity during an act of sexual coercion. A midwestern college student said, "I lost my virginity to a guy who forced me to have sex with him. He told me if we didn't have sex, he would make me use oral stimulation. I was too afraid to do either. I never saw him again even though we had been dating for awhile."

For some women, what they viewed as coercion when it happened, they later recognized as rape. This is the case for a 41-year-old woman from Washington. Now she recognizes that her boyfriend raped her twice.

"It happened in a car. He wouldn't take No for an answer. He had orders for Viet Nam and felt that he might not return home to the U.S. alive. He said, 'Aw, you just don't want me to have any fun.'

"I was 21 years old and a virgin. We were engaged. He had always been polite and respectful to me before. He was a religious person and knew I was religious and that I wanted to wait until we got married before we had sex. He knew I wanted to have children and be a good wife and mother," she said.

"The orders for Viet Nam made him go crazy. He forced himself on me. I had not wanted to go out with him again after that first time, but he had said that he was sorry, that it would never happen again. He even bought me a Bible," she added.

"I believed him. That's the only reason why I had gone out with him the last time. I felt very foolish afterwards when he raped me a second time. I never told anyone. I was over 21 so I thought that I would be laughed at because no one would believe me. I never trusted men very much after that."

This woman, like many others, remembered the incidents exactly how they occurred—what happened, what he did, where they were, how it felt. Yet, for some women, such as this woman from Boston, there's remembrance only of the feelings.

She said, "My first boyfriend coerced me into sexual contact many times. I can't really be specific because I don't really know how he did it. I just know that I'm left with feelings from that relationship of 'This is too much too soon.' I wish that I didn't have these experiences," she said, "back when I was 17 and 18 years old."

Confusing sexual experiences at an early age are not unusual. Both young men and young women, inexperienced and naive, explore sexual behavior with curiosity. Too often, however, these explorations are not mutually agreed upon and the young women comply under duress.

Intimidation and deception

For Jayne and her girlfriend, they were both 13 years old when they had their first encounter with sexual coercion.

Jayne and her friend were going out with two boys from their class at school. Having boyfriends was important to them as it was for many of the first year high school girls in their suburban school. The boys knew that Jayne and her friend often babysat together, and after several sessions of necking and petting, the boys asked the girls where they would be sitting that weekend.

The girls told them and that evening the boys came to the house. This continued for several weeks and the girls became more and more reluctant to tell the boys where they'd be, fearing that they might get caught. The boys, however, threatened to tell everyone in class that the girls were sleeping with them. While this was a lie, the girls didn't want to ruin their reputations, so they continued to let the boys visit when they babysat.

Then one evening, the boys brought beer, and after the girls had drunk some, the boys let in their friends. They told the girls to go in the other room and have sex with the other boys. When the girls protested, they again were told that if they refused, the boys would tell everyone in school that they had slept with all of these guys. And even though the girls did comply, the boys went ahead and told everyone in school about the encounter.

Did the girls tell their parents? Or anyone else about how they'd been set up? No. They didn't because they were afraid of being blamed and because they felt partially to blame for going along with the boys for awhile. Instead, they endured embarrassment and harassment for years afterwards, often seeing the boys around the neighborhood even after they were no longer in school together.

And while Jayne now, at age 23, recognizes this situation as rape, her friend still does not and refuses to discuss it at all with Jayne.

A California woman also wrote of her coerced sexual contact at the age of 15. She said that it happened over 30 times while she dated a man who was then 32 years old.

"He knew I was a virgin and assured me he didn't want to take my virginity, he just wanted to touch me. When I first suggested not letting him fondle me, he threatened me with exposure of what we were doing. The last two times I dated him, he had me totally undress and he held and caressed me. He was fully clothed and we were parked in his car."

Finally, she quit seeing him because she felt guilt-ridden with what he was doing and uncomfortable with the differences in their age. Although she wasn't raped, she was sexually abused—used— by a man who took advantage of her while she was legally underage.

But another woman from West Virginia did not escape coercive date rape. She wrote that her lover, a married man, would coerce her into having sex by threatening to tell her parents that she was seeing him. Since she was still living at home, she gave in. Eventually his threats led to rape, forced anal intercourse and sado-masochistic practices.

While the circumstances of sexual coercion in a dating relationship vary, always the woman feels used. Sometimes upset with herself for "letting this happen to me" and other times angry over being deceived, it can take a long while before the emotional wounds heal. Because of the subtleties, sexual coercion confuses women who sometimes wonder what happened. In relationships where sexual coercion is a recurring theme, the woman can become trapped in a vicious cycle of pain, humiliation and guilt which affects her self-esteem. As her self-esteem becomes corroded, she's less able to recognize that she deserves better from a relationship and therefore less likely to have the internal strength necessary to get out. The man, on the other hand, continues to use the situation to his advantage and often demands more from the woman the longer they date.

11

I'm Worthless
I Deserve to be Abused

One common denominator among dating-abuse survivors is low self-esteem. It is clearly an issue which affects the majority of women who contacted me. As I searched to learn more about the roots of this low self-esteem, I found that it comes primarily from the family and it is supported by society.

But first, let's look at how low self-esteem is played out in dating relationships. There are basically two types:
- women who believe *I Don't Deserve Better* and
- the *I'm Worthless* group.

I don't deserve better.

In this situation the woman's self-esteem is so low that she desperately needs someone—anyone—in order to feel that she is OK. The real problem centers around her lack of self-worth. If she's fortunate enough to meet and date a man who's decent, caring and emotionally secure, she'll have a chance to rebuild herself. But, if she picks up with a loser, she's extremely vulnerable for abuse. She's on a dating roulette wheel.

A 33-year-old California woman wrote, "I was 15 years old and

dating for the first time. Jim was 18, gorgeous, a real 'catch'—
especially for me, The Fat Kid. He said he was taking me bowling,
but instead he parked in a well-known 'lovers lane.' We were
kissing and touching, and then he pulled me down on to my back
on the front seat and pinned me down; he forced his way into me—
that hurt horribly, as did my head hitting the steering wheel."

During her dating years, this woman has been pushed, choked,
slapped and coerced into having sexual contact. But in spite of all
this she said, "It's the emotional abuse that's hardest to handle as I
have a chronic self-esteem problem and I find I put up with it
(abuse) because I have a hard time believing I'm good enough *not*
to put up with it."

I'm worthless.

Some women not only put up with abuse because they think
they don't deserve better, they actually believe that they're worthless. These women told of their self-destructive tendencies. Often
during a period of adolescent or early adulthood rebellion, women
with self-destructive tendencies cared little about the dates they
chose.

Elaine, a 27-year-old New Yorker, admitted to self-deprecating
behaviors. At the age of 19 she said, "I went on a real bender of
sleeping with low life. I was self-destructive. I hated myself."

Reflecting back on this period in her life, Elaine said, "I would
say that my experiences with dating abuse were something I went
looking for deliberately because of two factors. One, I genuinely
wanted to be loved and I was initially too open and too sexually
available. And two, I was really spoiling for a fight."

Another woman in her mid-40s wrote of incidents which occurred when she was in her 20s. Her boyfriend instructed her to
have sex with other men and she complied. She now believes that
her boyfriend was paid. She said, "I was attracted to men who
would eventually emotionally abuse, reject and abandon me. The
incidents of having sex with others and my boyfriend being paid for
it was a bit extreme, but back then I would do most anything, put
up with most anything, for fear of being rejected and abandoned
again. I just couldn't let go."

After an abusive marriage and a succession of abusive dating relationships, she's now been celibate for over ten years. Presently in therapy, she's recently run an ad in a singles magazine in the hopes of breaking the pattern.

She wondered, "It seems to me I have been told by men that I'm not worth much and I believed it subconsciously and set myself up time and time again by being attracted to men who would treat me this way. I'm still not sure if I can avoid Mr. Wrong. It worries me but I'm going to try very hard. The other thing I worry about is what if I do find Mr. Right? Someone who does treat me the way I want to be treated—will I recognize him? Will I appreciate it? Will I know how to act?"

Roots of low self-esteem

Low self-esteem and how it affects women in dating relationships has its roots in several areas. Most of the damage to the self-esteem begins in childhood, some of it is defaced by society, and another piece of the erosion comes from dating experiences.

Many women related their childhood experiences within dysfunctional families. Whether coming from homes with alcoholic parents, battering parents, or parents who emotionally neglected them, all of these women were left with the message that they weren't good enough. They believed that if they had been good enough they would not have been beaten, Mom or Dad would not have gotten drunk all the time, and they would have been loved more. Their overwhelming sense of loss—of love, nurturing, normalcy—during childhood was later acted out in painful scenarios of abusive-dating relationships.

A 44-year-old Massachusetts woman wrote, "I was sexually abused by my grandfather between the ages of 11 and 13. This consisted of fondling, getting into bed with him, etc. As an adult I have felt that I have abnormal confusion about sex. Specifically, I feel that I cannot say *No* and can easily be talked into doing things that at the same time I feel I shouldn't do, for instance, sex after a brief acquaintance."

She wrote that in one situation she was involved with a man she later learned was a convicted sexual offender.

Hunger for affection impacts on many women. The need to fill the void left from their parents'—mainly their fathers'—lack of warmth towards them led these women into relationships with anyone who'd give them a semblance of closeness. Since they never experienced real bonding with their fathers, how were they to differentiate abuse from love? Furthermore, if they had experienced physical or sexual abuse as children, this intermingling of abuse with love served to reinforce their notions, however misguided, that when someone purportedly loves you, you get hurt.

Childhood sexual abuse

Yet for some women, the abuse they suffered as children was clouded for many years in a sea of uncertainty. Sara, a 32-year-old woman from California, wrote that just recently she's been able to say that she was sexually molested by her father.

"Looking back on it now, I realize that I often felt uncomfortable with my father's physical affection, his holding me down and tickling me, or clinching me tight and covering my face with kisses, or wanting me to sit on his lap when I was in the 6th grade. He used to laugh over the fact that one time, when I was 10 or so, I shrugged him off and said, 'Don't do that. You have a wife of your own.'"

Later when she was 15 years old, her father would climb into her single bed with her. She found it annoying when he was sober, scary when he was drunk. Her father would also walk around the house naked even though she asked him not to and would walk into her room while she was in various stages of undress. Once he even pulled back the shower curtain claiming that he was looking for his wife, Sara's mother.

When Sara tried to talk to her mother about her father's getting an erection when he embraced her, her mother negated her feelings when she replied, "Oh, for gosh sake, do you really think that your own father wants to screw you?" Sara was too embarrassed to answer *Yes*. Then Sara told her mother's friend, a former teacher, that her father's actions made her nervous. The friend also invalidated her feelings by insisting that since Sara's father was a physician, seeing women undress wasn't the same for him as for other men.

Wondering if she was in fact "dirty-minded" as her mother had accused her, or heading for nymphomania because she experienced strong sexual urges, Sara entered into a relationship with the husband of her mother's friend. She said, "I felt guilty about it at the time, but I needed to know that I was sexually desirable to a man, *any man*. He did everything but sexual intercourse. I was 17; he was 55 years old."

For a Massachusetts woman, the connection between being sexually abused by her father and her later abuse by dates is quite clear. Paula said, "I was raped by my father when I was growing up so when I dated men I was used as a sex object. They bribed me into having sex and they kept saying if I didn't have sex with them they would tell my friends in school. They said I needed to keep it as a 'secret,' (This is what many fathers tell their daughters.) and if I told anyone, they would come back and kill me with a gun. So I shut my mouth and never said anything."

Paula continued, "They would take me out for a good time and then, in return for the good time, they wanted sex. I always gave in because I was afraid to say *No*. I had a broom handle put up my vagina which tore my insides and I have endometriosis from it." She understandably added, "Now I'm petrified of men."

Acceptance and expectation of abuse

All types of abuse in one's own family can lead to an acceptance and expectation of abuse in a relationship. Some women reported being ridiculed by family members because of their looks—being called fat, sloppy, lazy, pimply, worthless, stupid or ugly. Other women remember how their mother was abused and they, in turn, expected the same from their partners. Whatever the parameters of the abuse—physical, sexual, verbal, emotional—the results led to a downward spiral of diminishing self-esteem and self-worth.

When one thinks little of oneself, it follows that others should do the same. Women who've had a pattern of dating abusive men are generally women with a problem of low self-esteem. While they may or may not recognize that a certain situation or person is abusive, they often fall into another relationship with an abusive man. This is not to imply that they are masochistic, they clearly do not enjoy being abused. Instead, they don't realize that their misdirected subconscious beliefs lead them to—and keep them with—men who will abuse them.

Or, a woman from a dysfunctional family is so desperate to get away from home, that she considers any man she dates to be her Prince Charming. She builds him up as her way to escape an abusive homelife so that when he too becomes abusive, she's not equipped to accept that he's less than what she needs. In her fantasy of wanting to be loved and swept away, she continues to date an abuser.

These issues can be so imbedded in a woman's personality that even when she discovers the core of the problem, she has difficulty overcoming the trauma which caused her so much pain.

Thoughts of suicide

For Terri, a 28-year-old Sacramento woman, her life clearly changed at the age of 16 when she remembers herself as friendly, outgoing and trusting. Since that time she's lost her trust in others and often questions her ability to survive.

Terri was invited to a party and was subsequently raped by about fifteen men. "At 16, I was naive, a virgin and far too trusting. What hurt the most was the loss of belief that people were not out to hurt to me. I never thought that anyone would have that much viciousness," she said.

"Although I was traumatized and soulfully defeated, I tried to pretend that everything was fine. But I lost my enthusiasm and closed myself into a shell."

She never told her father, who had an alcohol problem, of the gang rape and only told her mother three years later. She described her mother's reaction as "No response."

"I ended up moving from my parents' home and became very promiscuous. I believe I felt that if I gave in I wouldn't have to be put through the terror."

But she was put through it again. Twice more she was raped: once by a man she met in a bar and once by a relative of her sister's husband. Although she's been in therapy for five years, Terri still gets panic stricken when someone speaks with her face to face. She said that she desperately needs to feel safe for a while in order to be able to forget a little bit of what happened to her.

Voice trembling, Terri told me, "If I could, I would kill myself, but I don't have the choice. I don't have the guts to kill myself and my body doesn't seem to want to die on its own."

Another woman also spoke of suicide. Erica, a 33-year-old professional woman from New York, traces her low self-esteem and subsequent dating abuse to the fact that she's an adopted child. Erica has spoken with other adopted children and said, "The theme of low self-esteem is very strong. A lot of adoptees feel that there must have been something wrong with them because they were given up. Even though the adoptive mother assures the daughter that there was nothing wrong with her, that the birth mother just couldn't keep her, the adoptee still believes that there was another reason for 'getting rid of me.'"

Erica said that she and her two adoptive siblings all have problems with feeling inadequate and unlovable. She said, "Part of it also had to do with my adoptive parents' style which was pretty cold and unaffectionate. So that when I became a teenager and I found that I could get affection in a different way, I was just really hungry for that."

When she began to date a man who gave her love and affection, she found that when the relationship turned abusive she couldn't end it because she was just too hungry for the romance. "I was willing to accept getting slapped around every couple of weeks, getting yelled at—he even tried to strangle me—and I still went out with him for a year after that."

In some ways she recognized that the relationship was very unhealthy but she just couldn't see a way out. On one occasion Erica was hit by her boyfriend on the front porch of her house. Her sister who witnessed the incident told their mother the next day. Her mother responded, "Oh well. She must have deserved it." It confirmed Erica's sense of hopelessness and entrapment.

Only many years later when Erica found her birth mother (Erica was 30 years old at the time) did she begin to claim her self-esteem. It gave her a feeling of strength which she had not had before. In fact, just three weeks after she had found her mother, she ended an abusive relationship she had been in for six months.

Erica said that if she had not found her birth mother she would have killed herself. "I was very depressed and suicidal at the time."

For women with low self-esteem, there's often lack of nurturing in their backgrounds. These women try to trust someone—a man—when they weren't given the opportunity at any early age to learn the difference between trust and mistrust. Instead they become progressively more insecure as they search for what's been missing—only to be abused again. Craving to be loved, fearing disappointment, and being alternately confused and abused, women with a low self-esteem must first heal their early wounds in order to progress to healthy adult-to-adult dating relationships.

12

Manipulating through Control and Jealousy

Abusive relationships consist of two people: the controller and the controlled. From the outside, the controller often appears Machiavellian, but his actions most probably come from his emotions rather than his intellect. This is not to imply that abusers aren't shrewd. They are. But their treachery lies more in their attitude, "I'm better than you are," than in their scheming.

For the women involved in these relationships, the lack of a clearly defined plot puts them at a disadvantage. Sometimes kind, caring and loving and other times nasty, jealous and violent, the abusers keep their dates dancing to a jumbled tune.

Unfounded and out-of-proportion suspicions

For a 38-year-old professional woman, her date's jealousy brought humiliation and pain.

Patricia said, "He used what he thought I did—sleep with someone—as justification for getting involved with someone else. His new relationship lasted almost a year before he got tired of her. Meanwhile, I was still trying to hang onto him—very humiliating and emotionally abusing."

A college student in her early 20s went through a similar period of jealousy with her boyfriend. Kelly said, "My boyfriend would ask around to find out if I had been partying during the week while he was in another city working. If he found out that I had gone out, he would ignore me by giving me the silent treatment and withholding affection the whole weekend."

Eventually, Kelly broke up with her boyfriend. She had the foresight to recognize that he, not she, was wrong.

But jealousy is often controlling and potentially violent. In fact, most men who are physically abusive towards women suffer from an overabundance of jealousy. They look for things to make them suspicious, then often invent reasons to be jealous.

When one New York woman was 17 years old, her date warned her of his potential jealous reaction. She said, "He told me that he didn't want me to even talk to anyone else who was male. Then, he smacked his fist into his hand for sound effects. I winced, because my natural reaction to loud noises was to do so. He laughed and teased me for weeks about how I was so afraid of him. He loved feeling more powerful than me and intimidating me."

She continued, "I thought he was harmlessly macho; I was wrong."

After their relationship cooled somewhat and she didn't care to date this guy anymore, she took a walk into town with another man. She said, "It was a beautiful day, and we chatted away and picked flowers. Suddenly, my former boyfriend screeched his car across the highway in front of us, stopping us in our tracks. My previous date jumped out of his car followed by two enormous men. He pushed the man I was walking with up against his car, all the time screaming and getting more red in the face.

"I cowered back into some shrubbery, afraid for my life—and for the man I was with. After a heated shouting match between the two men, the three guys piled into the car and screeched down the road. I felt like a stolen dog whose previous 'owner' was jealous of the second 'owner.'"

This sense of ownership continues to be operative in many relationships. Often starting with dating and later into marriage when one partner believes he owns the other, the "owner" becomes the controller.

Vengeance

Vengeance over a break-up in romance typifies the jealous, controlling type. Attempts to disgrace the woman—threats, displays and use of a weapon—are commonplace. A Chicago woman wrote, "A friend of mine had a relationship with a much older man. He was extremely possessive and accused her of sleeping with all of her male and female friends—including me. After they broke up, he followed her for months, sending massive 30-to 60-page letters outlining these imagined sexual infidelities. He sent one spectacularly nasty letter to her father documenting her alleged immoral behavior. If she had actually done everything he accused her of, she would never have had time for anything else!"

Many men behave normally until they realize that someone else finds their date attractive. Like a male dog protecting a bitch in heat, some men can't handle the notion that other men might want to date their women also.

One woman wrote, "I dated a man who thought he was doing me a favor by dating me. When he finally figured out that other men found me attractive, he couldn't handle it. At a party one night, I ran into some men friends that he didn't know. He came unglued and started calling me names and accusing me of picking men up from off the streets."

The jealousy gets so out of control at times that the men go from being unreasonable to outrageous. A New York woman remembered, "When angry, Gary would swear at me calling me things like 'whore,' 'bitch,' etc. I remember feeling that it was unfair because I was far from a whore. I didn't dare even look at men for fear that Gary would start something," she said.

"Once he even got mad at me because he 'caught' someone holding my hand in a bridal party procession. It was one of the ushers. Gary took me by the arm out to the parking lot and hit me and called me names and threatened my life if I even looked at the usher again during the evening. I was crying but when we went back into the catering hall, I had to pretend all was fine, or else!"

Insecure men

Yet, for other men the extent of their jealousy precedes the relationship entirely. Jealous and crazed over the thought that their women ever had sex with other men, these men often fly into rages.

An Ohio woman in her mid-20s had one such boyfriend. "My ex-boyfriend was very jealous of anyone I dated prior to him. He constantly wanted to know the number of people I had slept with before him, who, where, etc. I had been pregnant some years before and had given the baby up for adoption. He constantly belittled me for my pregnancy and choice (HA!) of the father of my baby. Verbal abuse was his specialty if things did not go his way. He constantly accused me of sleeping with others—primarily men that are very close friends of mine and with whom I have strictly platonic relationships. The possibility of two people of opposite sexes having a non-sexual relationship was more than he could comprehend."

The man who seeks to control his date has difficulty with his own self-esteem. Insecure with himself, he attempts to gain some semblance of security by creating a dependent relationship with a woman. This can be accomplished in a variety of ways. For many women, the control occurs because they are fearful of the man's ability to harm them. For other women, the control centers on more subtle behaviors.

A 25-year-old Indiana woman wrote of one such situation. "One man almost had me convinced I was crazy. He would tell me I had done things I knew I hadn't. I had friends check out his stories to find out if I was losing my mind. He later confided that if I thought I was crazy, I would be more dependent on him and could never be without him!"

Clearly it takes a strong woman, one with her own sense of self-esteem to thwart attempts to be controlled and dependent in a relationship. Ten years ago, a Virginia woman, now in her early 30s, ended a relationship when her partner demonstrated his ability to seriously hurt or kill her.

She wrote, "The breaking point came in 1977. We'd been out to a nice dinner at a French restaurant. Drove back to town and he got a room for us at a Holiday Inn. Nice full-length, seventh floor windows—and when I came out of the shower, dressed in a towel, hair still wet, he was standing there, fully dressed by the open curtains, holding a loaded .45. He ordered me to drop the towel! Threatened me with the gun! I got upset, didn't see any humor in it and flat out refused—told him he was scaring me. He quit his game, but I'd had enough. Haven't seen him in ten years."

Yet, this woman is one of the lucky ones who was able to call her date's bluff and remain physically unscathed. Other women are not as fortunate and have been subjected to force and violence.

A 25-year-old Ohio woman said, "One time my ex-boyfriend was yelling at me and was standing very close to my face. I put my hand on his chest to push him away from me repeatedly, and each time I would push him back, he would punch my right arm. He was a boxer and had a very healthy right hook!" she said.

"My arm was swollen, bruised and very close to being broken—all because I kept trying to push him away from screaming in my face. After I went to the doctor and had my arm x-rayed and my boyfriend realized he had hurt me, he was very apologetic—tears and all—trying to convince me he didn't mean it. Later, he tried to rationalize it to himself that if only I wouldn't have kept pushing him away and would have let him 'talk' to me, the whole incident wouldn't have happened."

Patterns of control

Once the pattern of control begins, it's unlikely to end of its own accord. Nonetheless, many women remain in controlling relationships because they fear reprisal if they try to end the relationship, believe that they can make the abuse end, or they feel powerless to do anything.

Joyce, a New Yorker now in her 40s, regreted her reaction after her boyfriend's first show of control. "I guess what hurt me the most was the very first time he slapped me. We were 14 and 15 years old and he was very jealous at my being at the shore with my family. He believed I was seeing other guys. I could not convince him and in a heated argument, he slapped me across the face. We were on a walking path in a park and someone else saw us. I remember being very embarrassed, then surprised, then hurt," she said.

"What bothers me most now is how for myself, my integrity, I was not angry enough to stop it there and then. I was mostly embarrassed that I was seen in this weak position," she said.

For Joyce, what began as a slap in the park, culminated in an eighteen-year abusive relationship. Married to this man for thirteen of those years, she said, "I also believe now my fate was being decided by my response to that first slap. How different would the next eighteen years of my life have been if I slapped him back or broke off with him, or just flat out said, 'Don't EVER do that to me again.' Instead, I accepted the slap, and the pattern began."

The pattern of control and jealousy continues and strengthens with the length of the relationship. Every woman who's been in this type of dating relationship regrets having stayed in it as long as she did. It only gets worse, never better. In hindsight the women view these relationships as a type of imprisonment—only worse because they were behind invisible bars.

Part Three

The Healing Process

13

Identifying the Wounds

The first consideration in the process of healing from dating abuse is to determine how you've been abused. While this may appear to be a senseless question, for many it's the crux of the issue.

Whenever I talk about dating abuse to a group, there are women who tell me that they never realized they had been abused in a dating relationship until they heard me identify how it manifests itself. Hearing the issues, listening to the stories of what happened to other women, and relating it to your own experiences is critical to the understanding of dating abuse.

When I read the completed questionnaires and interviewed women for this book, I became more in touch with the abuses I suffered from my dates. Incidents I had long forgotten, discounted or minimized were jarred loose from my memory. And when these pieces of my history flashed before me, I was forced to look at how they affected me in my current relationship and what I had done— if anything—to heal myself.

It's important to recognize *that* you've been abused and *how* you've been abused. Breaking it down into specifics, looking at questions and answering them both objectively and subjectively will give you a document to gauge the amount and severity of abuse you've suffered. As you look over and answer the questions on the next several pages, be honest with yourself. If you are not able to complete a question, come back to it later. One woman took weeks to fill it out. She said that she found the process difficult but therapeutic, and with the aid of her husband as a support person she completed it.

You too may need the assistance of a friend, partner or counselor. Take your time. Be kind with yourself and go at your own pace. As with all else, when the timing is right, you'll do it. And if the time is now, by all means proceed.

Dating Abuse Questionnaire

1. Physical

Has a dating partner ever

pushed or shoved you?	yes (# of times_____) __no
slapped you?	yes (# of times_____) __no
kicked you?	yes (# of times_____) __no
bit you?	yes (# of times_____) __no
punched you?	yes (# of times_____) __no
beat you?	yes (# of times_____) __no
choked you?	yes (# of times_____) __no
thrown things at you?	yes (# of times_____) __no
threatened you with a weapon?	yes (# of times_____) __no
physically abused you in some other way than the above?	yes (# of times_____) __no

106

Which incident(s) hurt you the most? What happened? You may want to write this down and talk about it with a trusted person.

2. Sexual

Have you ever been in a situation with a dating partner in which

    your date treated you like
      a sex object?   yes (# of times_____) __no

    your date coerced, bribed
      or tricked you into
      having sexual contact?   yes (# of times_____) __no

    you had sex because of
      what your date told you
      would happen if you
      didn't?   yes (# of times_____) __no

    you gave in to having
      sex for fear that your
      date would become vio-
      lent if you refused?   yes (# of times_____) __no

    your date used force or
      violence to get sex?   yes (# of times_____) __no

    your date sexually
      abused you in some
      other way than the
      above?   yes (# of times_____) __no

Which incident(s) hurt you the most? What happened? You may want to write this down and talk about it with a trusted person.

3. Verbal

Have you ever been involved with a date who hurt you by

putting you
   down?   yes (# of times_____) __no

swearing at you or calling
   you names?   yes (# of times_____) __no

demeaning you in front of
   others?   yes (# of times_____) __no

accusing you of things you
   didn't do?   yes (# of times_____) __no

exploding into a jealous,
   angry outburst over
   something that never
   happened?   yes (# of times_____) __no

threatening to harm you?   yes (# of times_____) __no

verbally abusing you in
   some other way than the
   above?   yes (# of times_____) __no

Which incident(s) hurt you the most? What happened? You may
want to write this down and talk about it with a trusted person.

4. Emotional

Have you ever dated someone who

regularly gave you the
   silent treatment?   yes (# of times_____) __no

would ignore you for
   periods of time?   yes (# of times_____) __no

would break promises and
   then deny it?   yes (# of times_____) __no

belittled your feelings?   yes (# of times_____) __no

intimidated you or made
   you feel fear?   yes (# of times_____) __no

led you to believe that
   there was more to the
   relationship than there
   was?   yes (# of times_____) __no

emotionally or mentally
   abused you in some other
   way than the above?   yes (# of times_____) __no

Which incident(s) hurt you the most? What happened? You may want to write this down and talk about it with a trusted person.

A guide for healing

Use this completed questionnaire as your guide through the healing process. Some incidents may have had minimal effect or none at all. If so, consider that a gift you have given yourself. But other experiences may still affect you, and in ways you're hardly cognizant of.

As we discuss the issues surrounding healing, keep in mind that it is possible to heal the wounds and to develop a close, trusting relationship with another person. It is also possible, but more difficult, to heal the wounds which have occurred in a current relationship. The difficulty lies in your partner's willingness to accept responsibility for what he's done to you, to want to change, and then to actually change his behavior. If both you and he are willing, it can be done and you can change an abusive dating relationship into a healthy one. Note that the change process is not yours alone. If he won't change, healing the wounds is a moot point. You can't heal wounds which are in the process of active infection.

14

Blaming the Victim/
Protecting the Abuser

Much, if not all, of what happens in dating abuse occurs because we are women—women living in a sexist society which condones and perpetuates abuse and violence against women. Yet, we as women tend to see what's happening to ourselves as a character defect. We blame ourselves for being flirtatious, having poor judgment, not being clever enough, and for trusting too much.

Because we tend to look inward for the causes of abuse against us, we believe what our confused minds are telling us. And as we believe that we are at fault for being abused, we become alienated from the one person we need to survive—ourself.

Conspiracy of silence

By not recognizing that dating abuse comes from the male culture of our society, we may put the blame not only on ourselves but on other women. If we haven't been abused, we wonder what that other woman did to get hurt so badly. And if we have been abused and have blamed ourselves for it, we must also blame the other women who've been abused for surely they too were the cause of it. This alienates us from other women; the very women who can validate what's happened to us.

Even when women are given clear warnings from other women that a man is a potential abuser, they often discount it. For Brenda, even when a former girlfriend of Daryl called to tell her that Daryl was violent, she didn't believe it. Instead she considered the former girlfriend jealous and petty. Only later when Brenda was nearly killed, did she recognize the kindness of the warning.

Women unknowingly band together in a conspiracy of silence. Embarrassed about what happened to us, fearful that no one would believe us, afraid of what our date would do if we went public with the tales of this abuse, and harboring the conviction of self-blame, women unknowingly contribute to the perpetuation of abuse against themselves and against other women.

One woman told me of her experience in college when she was dating a man, another college student, who nearly raped her. They were in her dorm room and the man pressed her for sex. When she declined, he became forceful and demanding. Fortunate to be able to fight off a potential rape, she refused to date him again.

"I really liked this guy until he did that to me. Now I shudder that I could have married someone who was a potential rapist," she said.

Yet, when a friend of hers started dating this guy, she did not tell her friend what had happened. She felt her friend would consider her to be acting out of jealousy. She also feared what her former date's reaction would be if her friend told him about their conversation. For her, as for many women, it was a painful decision to make because she wanted to protect her friend but she didn't know how.

Blaming the victim

In the end we diminish our own self-worth for the good of the abuser. We protect his image, give him permission to continue his ways—and feel guilty in the process.

Men also contribute to blaming us. Reinforcing our underlying fragility, they often tell us that we're the reason they abuse. Women have been called "frigid," "ice woman," "dyke" and a "baby" when they've refused to have sex. Conversely, we've also been attacked as being "prick teasers," "flirtatious," "too sexy," and "leading a man on." In short, when a man doesn't get what he wants sexually, he finds a way to blame the woman.

But other men blame women for abuses that don't involve sex. When one woman was punched repeatedly by her date, she was told that it was her fault for getting so close to him. Another woman showed her date the bruises he caused on her arms and legs, and her date denied he had done it. Instead he accused her of going out with someone else. And of course, there's the classic excuse of "I was only trying to calm you down" after a display of physical aggression.

A New Hampshire woman wrote of a relationship in which her partner blamed her for wanting intimacy.

"We were very attracted towards each other at first sight. The attraction was expressed after several drinks at a party in the form of intense kissing. As often happens in college, the affectionate exchange was blown off the next day as if nothing happened," she said.

But that set the tone for the rest of the relationship: intimate sexual contacts followed by a cold aloofness. When this woman confronted him on his behavior, her date concurred with her observation but didn't suggest any solutions.

She said, "I'll never forget how he once verbally acknowledged his attraction for me and explained how he wasn't ready for a relationship. It wasn't even a week later that he started a serious involvement with a woman from the same dorm. From that point on I felt as though I was the kind of woman he could sleep with but not the kind of woman he could bring home to mother—if that's how the cliche goes."

It was toward the end of the relationship that she felt the most abused. She said, "We had once again ended up together after an alcohol-filled evening. Right after having sex, he got up from the bed and sat beside it in a chair. It was obvious something was wrong, and after inquiring, he blurted out, 'How do you feel about abortion?' Trying to be calm, I pursued the meaning behind the question. He wanted to know if I thought or was concerned about getting pregnant, which I openly admitted to being very concerned. His response, 'Well, it certainly doesn't seem like it.' He then confessed to feeling guilty, and how I didn't deserve what was

113

happening. The discussion escalated to his angry departure."

She continued, "I cried intensely until the next morning, blaming myself for a number of things—for not being concerned about getting pregnant, for letting someone treat me that way, for letting him leave the way he did, etc.

"I can see now that I was being made responsible for things that he should've accepted as much—if not more—responsibility, but to this day it's hard to be with a man sexually without feeling ill at ease."

Still overcome with belief in some of his blaming, this woman has combined it with her own self-blaming and it is affecting her relationships with others. The nagging doubts, the "if only's" which stay with us, can hinder our growth from self-blaming to self-affirmation.

Self-affirmation is the belief that we do things for our own *good* not for our own demise. It is a *trust in ourselves that we do the best we can in any situation*, and *Yes, we will sometimes make a mistake*. But admitting to a mistake is not the same as blaming the victim.

- **Victim Blaming:** "It's all my fault the relationship ended. I should have been more available to him. I should have paid more attention to him. If only I had tried harder, he wouldn't have stood me up."
- **Admitting a Mistake:** "I guess I was wrong when I thought that he cared as much about me as I did about him."

When you can admit a mistake without blaming yourself for what your date did to you, you're off the victim-blaming trek and on the road to self-affirmation.

Many women make a *little* mistake and take on a *lot* of victim blaming. This is particularly true of women who have been date raped.

A 27-year-old Maine woman wrote, "There were about thirty people in this very specialized course, and most of us socialized together. I gave Pat a ride home from a party one night and went in to his house to use the bathroom. When I walked back in to the kitchen to leave, he started grabbing at me. I kept saying *No*. Pretty soon he was throwing me into the walls, onto the floor, dragging me away from the door and also trying to push me through another door to his bedroom. It was midwinter so I had a long, wraparound knit scarf on that he pulled tightly around my neck several times.

"Eventually his roommate came out to see what was going on, so Pat cooled it somewhat but still wouldn't let me leave. The roommate went back to bed (Note: this is part of the *male* conspiracy of silence.) and Pat started up again. This had been going on for 30 to 45 minutes and I was tired of it, but I was feeling guilty that I wouldn't let him!

"I gave up the struggle and let him push me to his room. I did a starfish impression and cried when he was done. He actually asked me what was wrong! Did this guy believe we'd just been through a normal mating ritual? He made me stay till morning."

She continued, "This happened seven years ago and up until a few months ago I still laid a lot of the blame on myself. I shouldn't have given him a lift, I shouldn't have gone in . . . blah, blah, blah. Finally, as I was explaining to a young woman who had been abused by a stranger when she was a child that it wasn't her fault, it occurred to me that it wasn't my fault either. Someone who I thought was a friend betrayed me and turned out to be an asshole and a rapist. I think I'm finally getting over it."

Did she make a mistake by giving this man a ride? In retrospect, yes. But certainly at the time there was no way for her to know that this guy would rape her. Her decision to give him a ride was based on her acquaintance with him and her belief and trust that he was a decent person. Without clues to indicate otherwise, how can she be to blame for giving him a ride?

Victim blaming often involves stretching the events which led up to the abuse into an unrealistic notion of what we should have anticipated. We lay a heavy burden upon ourselves that we should have anticipated what would happen—even though there is no humanly possible way that we could have foreseen it.

Healing the wounds of self-blame means that we first have to stop blaming ourself. When we can recognize that even though we made a mistake or used poor judgment, no one has the right to hurt us, and we can begin to redirect ourselves toward self-affirmation.

It is important to find a person who will listen to your nagging self-blame, someone who will hear your doubts and will ask you the questions needed to rid it from you.

Find a person—friend, partner, counselor—who can ask

- How were you to know that if you went into his apartment he'd try to rape you?

- What do you think your date's responsibility was in this situation?
- So you had a few drinks and said some mean things, does that give him the right to hit you?
- It takes two people to make a relationship work and you've only told me how you ruined it. What was his part in it?

When you have someone who will listen to you first, then ask you crucial questions, you eventually will begin to lessen your feelings of self-blame. And in time, you will ask yourself these same questions whenever you find that you're accepting more blame than the situation merits.

15

Psychological Scars/ Emotional Pain

As with most life crises, the lingering effects of dating abuse center on emotional trauma. This is not to minimize the physical damages which can leave permanent losses. Certainly any long-standing physical impediment requires care and treatment for the survivor to overcome, but in the end, it's generally the emotional pain which outlives the physical. Even when the physical pain subsides and the survivor is left with a limp, a scar or the inability to bear children, what she endures is a constant reminder of an extremely painful occurrence in her life.

Sixth sense for survival

For many women, there's phenomenal clarity in their remembrance of what happened. Details regarding her date, what he wore and how he looked are as clear as her memory of what he did to her. Women have recounted the sequence of events to long and grueling date rapes, kidnappings and beatings. Along with what was inflicted on them, they often remember finer details: the color of the walls, how the furniture was placed, what covered the floors.

Dating-abuse survivors are not unusual in this respect. Overall, trauma victims manifest excellent recollection of their ordeal for, often, when people are in life-threatening situations their perceptions heighten. It's as if the body adds a sixth sense to aid us in survival. The fear and panic of impending harm or death, coupled with the realization of not being physically strong enough to ward it off, set the mind into motion to serve as the protector.

For some of the women I spoke with, this extra sense is what freed them from the hands of a date rapist. Even while their body was being abused, their mind continued to plot ways out, and when the first plan didn't work, their mind found another way to escape.

One women insisted that her date who had just raped her let her go to the bathroom. She told him that she'd have no choice but to urinate and defecate on him if he didn't. While in the bathroom, she planned her escape, calculating the layout of the apartment and how many steps to the door. Yet, when she came out of the bathroom, it was pitch black and he grabbed her immediately. Her first plan thwarted, her mind plotted another.

Eventually she was able to convince him that she needed her diaphragm which was in her car. She put her coat on over her naked body and ran through the snow to her car. He followed her and got into the car. But still her mind took control. She talked him into driving to her dorm and insisted that he let her go in because she was signed out and needed to return at a specific time or the housemother would send someone out to look for her. She convinced him that the dorm staff knew she was out in front because they could recognize her car. After promising to go out on a date with him again, he let her go.

Other women reported similar scenarios. Some women were successful in warding off the date rape itself, others were date raped and then succeeded in getting out of the situation and away from further harm. But even when the details are remembered and women regain some control over the situation, the emotional elements remain. Control over where we are, who we're with, and what we do doesn't outweigh control over our emotions.

I've identified six major emotional issues which surfaced from the women who contacted me. Some women were physically abused, others sexually assaulted. Most suffered from verbal abuse. All were subjected to emotional abuse.

Some women spoke of several interrelated emotional and

psychological problems, others of just one. In separating and addressing each of these problems, I hope to give women an opportunity to recognize their own issues so that they can better focus on the crux of their emotional pain.

Fear for safety

Many women reported that they feared for their own lives after an incident of dating abuse. Often, the survivors of date rape and physical assault spoke of longstanding emotional problems.

For Marilyn, the woman who was nearly choked to death when she attempted to break up with Jim, it was nightmares. When she dated Jim, who physically abused her, she felt trapped. "I spent many nights in tears. I felt locked up somewhere, like I'd never get out," she said. Her fear was so great that when Jim asked her to marry him, she agreed. "I figured that I'd never get away from him anyway."

Eventually Marilyn found the strength to end the six-year relationship. But being away from Jim didn't end her pain. She suffered violent nightmares with Jim appearing in her dreams trying to hurt her. The nightmares continued for seven years. And during that time she feared dating others because of the potential for abuse.

This fear of abuse from other dates is common. While we all build our beliefs on what we've experienced in life, a survivor of dating abuse—particularly of sexual and physical abuse—often fails to recognize that the problem rests with the abuser. Instead, the woman internalizes what's happened as a problem with herself and assumes that it will happen again. This serves to intensify her fear of dating.

For Terri, the woman who was gang raped at age 16, then raped again two more times, the similarity she found in the rapes was that all of the guys had been consuming alcohol. Now for her own protection, she won't go out with anyone who drinks. But in reality, she rarely goes out with anyone. Fearful of any stranger, Terri freezes emotionally whenever someone speaks to her. It's as if her emotions went into hibernation in order to spare her the pain.

Even though fear can be an immobilizer, it also can be a healthy element. When fear is used to make one more cautious and more aware of the surroundings—people, places, things—then it can become a preventive tool. Fear doesn't need to be eliminated in order to heal the wounds. It does need to be reframed into a positive element rather than a debilitating one.

Loss of trust of self

Clearly one of the major issues dating-abuse survivors confront is lack of trust in themselves. Doubt in their own sense of whom to date, whom to trust, and what is safe further contributes to their self-blame. And when it's taken to the extreme, if you can't trust yourself, who can you trust? Thus, the dating-abuse survivor can feel hopeless.

When self-trust is missing, a woman becomes more vulnerable to abuse. Because she believes she has poor judgment, she makes bad judgments about the men she dates. In a sense, her life becomes a self-fulfilling prophecy. What she fears will happen does happen. And as she dates more men who abuse her, she's more convinced that she has poor judgment and can't trust herself.

For Bonnie, a New York woman in her early 30s, her self-fulfilling prophecy was being treated as a sex object. Although she hated it, "There were hundreds of times when I dated men who treated me as no more than a piece of meat, something needed to meet mere biological need. These experiences all seem to coalesce into one major nightmare in my memory."

Losing trust in oneself often is tandem to losing trust in others. Bonnie wanted her dates to treat her as a person, not a sex object. When her judgment proved wrong, she lost her ability to trust herself which resulted in a string of abusive dates.

Lack of trust in others

Besides a lack of trust in oneself, another common theme is the lack of trust in others. Clearly this is understandable since dating relationships involve intimacy, closeness and trust. When that intimacy is violated, the trust dissipates. And for many women, the trust transfers over to other men.

For Martha, the woman whose fiancé raped her and then gave her a Bible, after her fiancé raped her a second time she said, "I never trusted men very much after that." And although she didn't need any more reasons not to trust, at the age of 24 she was almost raped by another date. She said, "I got out of the car and got away. I have avoided men who drink ever since."

Some women's fear and mistrust of men co-mingle. One woman wrote, "The most awful, hurtful memory I have is from when I was in the service. I went out with my roommate on a blind date. It was a fiasco. We were driven to the mobile home these two guys shared. My roommate's date passed out, so this jerk I was with decided he was going to make it with both of us. My roommate managed to escape and walked two-and-a-half miles back to base. I was forced repeatedly and physically to suck this jerk off. I was able to prevent more narrowly defined rape—(vaginal penetration)."

She continued, "By way of context, I quit seeing men as dating and/or sex partners nearly eight years ago when I left the military. I remained celibate for seven of those years save for one fleeting sexual encounter with a man that finally convinced me that there was nothing positive in sexual relationships with men for me."

Now involved in a lesbian relationship, she said that men aren't the reason she's lesbian. But she said, "Men are the reason I will never involve myself sexually, physically or emotionally in a heterosexual bonding."

Like this woman, other women also have not been able to date for periods of months or years. One woman reported that it took three years before she could date again.

Sally was engaged to a man who repeatedly put her down, called her names and demeaned her in front of others. She said, "He unwillingly became engaged to me so that he could move into my house, have sex and be taken care of. Then he said that he never loved me and wouldn't marry me. He was always emotionally obtuse and abusive."

For Sally, the emotional and verbal barrage didn't begin until they had become engaged. She now sees some of it in relation to their differences. "Our backgrounds were entirely and dangerously different. He was the child of immigrants who inherited a lot

121

of inappropriate and highly angry class hatred and jealously and insecurity. I've learned and I'm more perceptive of people now, but I couldn't date anyone at all for three years afterwards."

For some women, the mistrust takes the form of anger towards all men. One woman wrote, "I do not trust men at all. They're either liars or emotionally retarded or sadists." When women have multiple experiences as those shared in this book, it's understandable that they may take on a negativistic view of the male species.

But this type of mistrust is unhealthy. It harbors constant anger and continual fueling of negative feelings. Your energy is consumed and you cannot become whole when this heavy baggage is carried around.

Lack of trust in others doesn't just mean not trusting men. Some women wrote of the pain they felt because they believed that they were set up by women friends. Another woman lost trust in her sister who blamed *her* when she was raped by the sister's husband. Many women told of loss of trust in parents who discounted their pleas for help when they were being abused.

Can mistrust of others be healthy? Most definitely—when it is put in a proper perspective and is used to prevent further abuse.

Self-esteem

As we've seen in another chapter, the lack of self-esteem contributes to remaining in an abusive relationship. But self-esteem is also destroyed as a result of an abusive relationship. And mending it can be a long and arduous process.

For some women, they clearly identify that their self-esteem was intact prior to the abusive-dating relationship. Before dating, they remember themselves as outgoing, happy and confident. After the dating abuse, they lacked confidence, questioned their abilities and felt worthless.

In light of the fact that dating abusers tend to put down their partners, demean them and treat them as inferior, it's understandable that a woman who experiences a dose of this would also begin to doubt herself. As people, we all need some outside validation to confirm our inner feelings of self-worth. When we begin to doubt ourselves, and if our outside environment feeds into this self-doubt and fuels it with self-degradation, we are at risk for low self-esteem.

One woman wrote how she recently recognized that she's too complying in relationships. This results in giving up her own needs and wants. When she talked this over with her mother, she found a clue. "My mother reminded me of one of my past boyfriends. Before I dated him, I was self-confident and strong. While dating him, every time I displayed any negative feelings he would shut me out and/or leave me. The thought of losing him scared me so much I would shut up and do things his way."

Another woman wrote, "I have a chronic self-esteem problem and I find I put up with abuse because I have a hard time believing I'm good enough not to put up with it." Again the self-fulfilling prophecy gives credence to what is happening. She started with low self-esteem and with each abusive incident, her self-esteem sank a bit lower.

When our self-esteem is good, we have the ability to recognize that it's being challenged. That's what happened to Nancy who recognized that her partner's put downs and threats were becoming extremely damaging. She wrote, "I know the difference between constructively criticizing someone and dissecting her according to your own point of view. I finally realized that I had to get out of the relationship before my self-esteem was destroyed."

Can low self-esteem ever be healthy? No. Mistaken for modesty or humility, some people would like women to believe that low self-esteem is a virtue and high self-esteem is equal to arrogance and snobbery. But in reality, self-esteem is what gives us our value in our self-worth. With a high self-esteem, we feel good about ourselves, our abilities and our decisions. It builds confidence—not arrogance.

Depression, addiction, suicide

Several women spoke of depression which followed dating-abuse relationships. The roots of depression are anger. And the anger results in depression when it is internalized rather than externalized. It's understandable therefore, why dating-abuse survivors would become depressed believing that they are to blame, that nothing will change, that they'll always meet losers.

Some women spoke of being in therapy or being hospitalized for depression. Other women spoke of extreme senses of loss and hopelessness which led to thoughts of suicide.

Women often have underlying rage in *normal* circumstances. Being born female into a male culture and treated as inferior from day one gives women reason for their rage.

Because our social structure gives women so many reasons to be angry and so few outlets to vent their anger, it is easy to see why women who've been abused in dating relationships often consider suicide. The dating myth after all supports the wonderful fantasy of falling in love, being taken care of, and a chance at a lifetime of happiness. Instead when a woman experiences emotional, physical or sexual pain, the turmoil becomes insurmountable.

Some women allow their depression to self-destruct. Not able to commit suicide, they become candidates for addiction: to drugs, to alcohol, to food, to smoking, to love. Whatever it takes to hide the wounds and mask the scars is what the depressed/angry survivor feels she *needs* to do. What results then is that *anger* runs her life. And yet, because she has suppressed her anger, she's not aware of it. And if she's not aware of it, she can't change it.

Love addiction, or the incessant need to have someone—anyone—to date is common with dating-abuse survivors. Often used as a way to ward off depression, love addiction exchanges one unhealthy element for another. In love addiction, women put up with abuses because they are not able to accept being without a relationship. Many women told of going on self-destructive binges, sleeping with dates because they wanted—needed—to feel close to someone.

When a woman can identify that she's addicted and that her addiction is a mask for depression, she's beginning to uncover the roots of the problem. Depression covered by addiction is dangerous. But depression which can be worked through with the help of a professional can bring a woman new insights and strength.

16

Evaluating Your Healing Process

The healing process in any life crisis is a fluid one. There are moments when we feel as though we've rid the pain from our lives and other times when the hurt surfaces and seems to overcome us. Progressions and regressions are part of the process and the goal is to build on the progressions and use the periods of regression to your own benefit.

To understand where you are in the healing process, you need to ask yourself some questions. An honest, soul-searching response will give you some clues about the issues which you still need to resolve. As with any healing process, it's important to be gentle with yourself. If the pain surfaces, don't blame yourself for not doing better. Accept it and use it to learn more about who you are.

Decide what you want to do with the pain now that you recognize it.

- Should you keep it as it is?
- Should you rid yourself of it by getting help from a couselor or trusted friend?
- Should you reframe it by accepting what you've learned from it?

As you read through the following questions, you may need to focus on one specific relationship or incident. Work through all of the questions with that relationship or incident in mind. When you feel as though you've finished, then begin on another relationship or incident. In this way you will be able to zero in on specifics which will aid you in ridding yourself from that "All Men Are Jerks" attitude.

Where are you in the healing process?

1. Identify the incident you're relating to. Who was it with? What happened? Where were you?

Remembering the facts will help you to relate to what you've experienced. Take time to recall the details of what happened and how it happened. Fill out the questionnaire from Chapter 13. You may also want to keep a journal of your thoughts and feelings while you work through this. Some women find it helpful to record their thoughts on tape. Use whatever serves you in identifying the details of what happened.

2. What was the most painful aspect of what happened? Was it physical injuries? Emotional hurt? Feelings of loss?

All aspects of pain are important to recognize but sometimes we forget to get to the nugget of that pain. Is it the slap in the face that stung—or the humiliation which accompanied the slap? Is it because he belittled you in public—or because he put you down in the first place?

What is the residue in your emotions that continues to cause you pain? Clearly, physical pain will hurt you. But when the pain subsides that doesn't mean that the hurt disappears. Often when the physical distress diminishes, it is replaced by emotional and psychological pain.

3. How do you feel about your behavior during the time you were being abused? Do you believe that you did the best you could?

A woman who was coerced and forced into having sex when her boyfriend pushed her onto a pool table reported that she later felt humiliated. She said, "I felt like shit, really worthless. It would have been so easy and ultimately so good for me if I'd used every physical and verbal weapon at my disposal." But she didn't and now she feels that she let herself down.

If you have similar feelings, you need to be gentle with yourself. Remember, you did not ask to be abused. Someone you knew and trusted hurt you. He had no right to do that. Your behavior during that time was based on what was happening then. You're assuming that you should have known what was going to happen. In reality, you didn't know because you couldn't have known. You did the best you could given the circumstances.

4. How are you functioning in the various aspects of your life: home, work, school?

If you are in a period of regression where you can't fulfill your daily obligations, you may gain comfort from knowing that other women have been there too. One woman wrote that she became a hermit for a week following a physical attack by her boyfriend. Other women indicated that they were hospitalized for psychiatric treatment because of dating abuse. While these may seem extreme, it's important to understand that each of us needs to heal in our own way. When a period of recluse becomes excessive, then it's time to reach out and get help. But if you need a day or several to hibernate, allow yourself the time.

For those of you who are continuing to function in your respective roles, you may be farther along in the healing process or you may be able to compartmentalize your pain. You perform your duties as employee or student separate from your personal life. Later, you may come home and emotionally let down. If you do this, it's your way of coping by allowing the pain to surface when you feel safe (at home) and keeping it in check at other times (at work or school). Don't belittle yourself with comments like, "But I do so well at school, why can't I be strong at home too?"

Clearly, whenever and wherever you feel the pain, it's because you need to do that in order to work through it. If you deny it, it won't go away. It may hide out for awhile but it'll be back. It's best to recognize the pain and let it surface. If it's too painful to deal with alone, seek help from others.

5. Are you taking care of yourself? Do you want the best for yourself?

Do you care how you look? What are you eating? Are your

grooming habits the way they used to be? In short, do you care about yourself and what's happening around you?

It's easy to give up on ourselves when we've been abused. Some women consider suicide or fall into depression, particularly after a series of abusive incidents or when someone they've been extremely intimate with abuses them.

This is understandable in light of the mourning process that many women suffer. Like the elements of a divorce, a dating-abuse survivor wonders what went wrong, what she did to cause this to happen, will it happen again with someone else, is there any hope? Her doubts and fears can lead to a sense of defeat. And why take care of yourself if there's no reason to?

Not taking care of oneself can include eating disorders such as bulimia, anorexia nervosa, overeating and other addictions such as alcohol, drugs, sex, tobacco. If you're feeling driven by something outside of you, you should seek treatment for help in regaining your ability to care for yourself.

As you pull up from this negative attitude, you'll find that you feel better about yourself and others. You'll feel more in control of your life. And when in control of your life, you're capable of taking care of yourself in healthy ways. When you safeguard yourself in your own environment, you feel more confident about safeguarding yourself elsewhere.

6. What have you done about your anger over what's happened? Have you allowed yourself to feel it? Release it?

So often, women lock up anger or redirect it so it won't be felt. If you haven't felt angry about being abused, take another look. Did you make excuses for what he did to you? Did you blame yourself for what happened?

If you haven't felt your anger and released it, you may need to do so in order to move on into a healthier space. Women's anger can be frightening because we so often store it up. Along with the anger over dating abuse may be rage over other earlier issues: childhood physical or sexual abuse, lack of emotional warmth and support from our parents, past unresolved incidents of dating abuse. Because of this, it's advisable not to go through it alone. Get help from someone supportive and trusted.

7. How do you feel about your current choice of dates? Do you trust men?

If you're dating a man who's abusing you, please ask yourself *why*? Is it because of how things used to be when the relationship was good? Do you feel sorry for him? Do you keep hoping he will change? Do you fear being without a relationship? Do you think you deserve abuse?

Making excuses for her date is one reason that keeps a woman in an abusive relationship. She claims that he acts the way he does because he had a bad childhood, or because some other woman jilted him, or because he drinks. When she makes excuses, she takes the responsibility off of him and places it somewhere where neither one of them have control over it. This results in the guy continuing to operate in an abusive manner with the woman staying in the relationship.

Or are you currently not dating because you don't trust men at all? Certainly, this is understandable given what you've experienced. Working through the healing process, however, means that you are able to differentiate what happened to you as an act that another person—or persons—did to you. It's something you can learn from, grow from, and use in avoiding potential abusers.

If you've gotten out of one abusive relationship and into another one, again ask yourself *why*? What's the same about these relationships? How are these guys alike? What attracted you to both of them?

You aren't alone if you've had a series of abusive partners; many women have been in the same situation. The issue isn't that you want to be abused; it's that you want to be loved. You want the good stuff: the caring, romance and closeness that comes with a relationship. But why do you pick an abuser? The answer may lie in the next question.

8. How do you feel about yourself? What do you like about yourself? What do you dislike? Do you trust yourself?

The way you feel about yourself can mean the difference between safeguarding yourself and becoming self-destructive. Numerous women told of how they purposely dated "low-life" because they hated themselves. Again, the self-fulfilling prophecy prevails: "I am no good, so I date men who will abuse me, and then

129

they can confirm that I am no good."

One of the things to consider here is how your date's behavior affects the way you feel about yourself? Have you felt different since you've known him? Do you feel less competent? Or more competent?

Women often see themselves reflected in their partners. What reflection comes back from him? How does he project *you* back to you? How does he project you to others? And how do you feel about that?

How your date *sees* you is a critical factor in how you see yourself in that relationship and in other parts of your life. One woman told of how she was on a self-destructive binge of dating abusive men. Then, she met the man she was eventually to marry. She said, "I thought that if he could love me when he's so nice, wonderful, lovely and smart, then I must be okay." It was the turning point in her life and her self-esteem began to grow.

When you don't feel good about yourself and have a low sense of self-esteem, you don't feel that you deserve much. You tend to date guys who put you down and abuse you in various ways. Because your opinion is low and you don't trust yourself anyway, you have little reason to get out of the relationship. After all, you'll just turn around and date some other jerk. Right?

Wrong. If you work on feeling good about yourself, believing in your right to be respected, you will not settle for someone who demeans and abuses you. It sounds simple, but it can work. Read "The Dating Woman's Bill of Rights" in the Affirmation section of this book every day until you believe every part of it.

17

Getting Help

Often when we are in crisis or in need of change in our lives, we want someone to fix it. Willing to turn ourselves over to a magical cure, we long for simplicity, for a cure with no pain attached. Unfortunately, this is not realistic. When we ceased being infants and young children, we left behind the ability of someone else to "make it better." As adults, young or mature, our happiness and ability to be happy centers on ourselves.

Know yourself.

The first step in helping yourself is to recognize who you are from the inside.
- What kind of a person are you?
- How do you feel about yourself?
- Do you like yourself?
- What do you want to change within yourself?

Notice that these issues focus on *you*. They don't center on who you're with, who you're dating, what your job is, or what style clothes you wear. The external elements of your life certainly have an effect on you, but they don't constitute *you*.

You can get a grasp on who you are in several ways. If you spend some time answering these questions, you'll begin to understand yourself better. You can write out the answers, talk to yourself in a mirror, or talk into a tape recorder and play it back. Allow for some undisturbed time to get reacquainted with yourself. Consider unplugging the phone.

1. How would you describe yourself if you were leaving a record to be included in a time capsule?
- What are your likes?
- What are the things you're the most of proud of?
- What are your hopes and dreams?
- What material things would you put in a time capsule?
- How would you describe what these items mean to you?

2. How would a friend describe you?
- Imagine that you are one of your friends. What would this friend say about you to another person?
- What would your friend say about your strengths?
- Your weaknesses?
- What is it about you that your friend especially likes?

3. Who would you be if you were transported to another part of the world right now?
- Imagine that you are standing in the middle of London, England. You have ample money in your pocket, the ability to speak the language, and all the time in the world. What would you do?
- Would you find some other people to connect up with? Or would you relish the solitude?
- Would you begin to explore the city? Or get out to the country? Or would you get to the airport and catch the first plane home?

4. Finish each sentence.
- I am most happy when—
- I get so angry whenever—
- The silliest thing I ever did was—
- I cry whenever—
- I get scared when—
- My biggest fear is—

- When I walk into a room of strangers, I—
- Happiness is—
- The one thing I won't tolerate is—
- Waking up in the morning is—
- At night I like to—
- When I'm alone I—
- My most embarrassing moment was—
- Someday I hope to—
- The thing I most admire about myself is—
- One thing I want to change in myself is—
- I hope I never—

When you begin to get answers to the question *Who Am I?*, you will move from *identifying* to *understanding*. The process will take you from describing your traits—strong/weak; happy/sad; attractive/plain; shy/outgoing; country person/cosmopolitan; dependent/independent; trusting/mistrustful—to understanding how those traits were developed.

In recognizing where the elements you are comprised of come from, be honest with yourself. Do you consider yourself plain because that's what you were told when you were a child? Are you mistrustful because of an abusive incident?

As you uncover who you are and where it all came from, recognize that you are who you are because of what you've experienced. Take the time to appreciate the strengths you've acquired along the way. Trust that you developed these traits for a reason and that your reasons were to take care of yourself. And remind yourself that you can overcome your less favorable traits. Know that you can use your past experiences to make yourself smarter.

One woman who had a string of abusive dating relationships recognized that she needed to foster independence in herself. After working on developing this trait, she learned how to be independent by believing in herself. This gave her the self-confidence she needed to recognize and avoid abusive dates.

Although the process of getting help begins with yourself, it doesn't mean that you have to do it alone. When you recover, the memories it can be painful. And the pain can hurt as much now as it did when the abuse occurred. For this reason, many women choose professional guidance in order to aid them through the process. There are many places to turn to for help.

Professional counseling

Finding a counselor or therapist can be both simple and complex. First there's the decision of the type of professional you want to see. You might choose between a social worker, psychiatrist, psychologist, pastoral counselor, psychiatric nurse or certified mental health counselor. All of these are professionals who have received extensive training. Besides holding a degree in their field, many have also studied in institutes or advanced training programs.

There is such a variety of therapists, both in types of degree and technique, that making a decision can be overwhelming. And no one therapy works the best for all people.

Some women report that they've been hospitalized for psychiatric problems stemming from dating abuse. One woman who told of a relationship in which she was grossly sexually and emotionally abused was hospitalized for seven months afterwards. Although hospitalization is not the norm for most survivors of dating abuse, if needed, it should not be ruled out. For this woman, her treatment program gave her the opportunity to break the cycle of needing people who hurt her. It gave her a new freedom.

Another woman from California who has been involved in a series of abusive relationships over a period of 12 years wrote, "In closing, after reading all this shit I lived through, I want to say that I have been in therapy for the last 5 years and I have learned a lot about me and life. I tend not to get used as often and have found power in myself. I can speak up and tell someone that they offend me by doing or saying something. I really am a new person, even though I know I still have problems to work out."

Counseling can help you process your personal and interpersonal feelings. It can aid you in looking at your dreams, fears, defenses and coping mechanisms. You may be able to recover memories from early formative years and the pain of a lost childhood. Counseling can also help you understand the systems you live in and with which you interact. It can give you tools to understand yourself and others and how it all is interwoven.

Being in therapy does not have to mean years of counseling. Some women work through issues over a period of weeks or months. In fact therapies such as crisis intervention and brief counseling focus on long-term gains in a condensed time period.

For the dating-abuse survivor, being in therapy means recovering the memories and releasing the anger. When the memories and anger remain inside of you, they inhibit you from developing healthy relationships—with yourself and others. Releasing the anger means being vulnerable to pain. And that vulnerability is why you may need the safety which counseling affords.

Your counselor or therapist must be someone you can trust. If you can't trust your therapist, then you won't work through the process of healing. For this reason, when you make the decision to see a counselor or therapist, you probably don't want to look up a number in the Yellow Pages. Instead, talk to people you know who've been in therapy. Ask them who they saw and what they liked about the person. If you don't have someone who can refer you to a counselor, then look up a number to a women's helpline or hotline. Explain that you've been abused by your date and want a referral to a counselor who is sensitive to these types of issues.

When you get your referral, check out the fee arrangement so that you have that cleared from your mind before you begin. You don't want to start seeing someone only to find out that you can't afford that person. Ask about insurance coverage and see if your plan will cover it. Some therapists charge on a sliding-fee scale, so you would pay according to your income. Others allow for some of their clients to receive free services.

The issue of selecting a male or female therapist is certainly a valid one. What's important here is that your therapist believes you, understands you, and supports you. Your best chance of getting these three components in a therapist is to choose a feminist therapist. There are other excellent therapists who are supportive to women's issues without labeling themselves "feminist." But make sure that whoever you eventually see in counseling is supportive to you as a person and as a woman. The last thing you need is a counselor—male or female—who adds to your sense of self-blame.

When you find your therapist or counselor, you will want to

know the person's credentials and his or her style of therapy. Ask the counselor where she trained, how long she's been in practice, and what style of therapy she does. If you don't understand the answers, ask for more clarification. But even more important than relying on your therapist's background and technique, begin to trust yourself. How do you feel? Does the therapist exude empathy? Does she seem to understand you? Care about you?

If you aren't comfortable with your therapist, acknowledge it. This is a chance for you to practice being assertive. You don't need to sit idly by while you sizzle inside. And if you and the therapist can't work out the issues between yourselves, you may need to find another counselor who will give you the safety and empathy you need in order to heal. Above all, your counseling experience should be a positive one. It's up to you to assure that it is.

Support group

A support group is similar to counseling in that you are understood, supported and believed. But unlike counseling, the support group provides you with a group of people who, like yourself, feel a sense of disequilibrium.

The support group generally centers on a specific topic or group of people. For example, an agency may sponsor a group for single women, another group for single parents, a third group for women who've been sexually assaulted, etc. In order to identify what group would work best for you, call a women's helpline or hotline in your community. Explain your circumstances and ask what's available. Find out if there is a support group for survivors of dating abuse and if not, suggest that one be started.

Be aware that a support group does not offer counseling in the sense than an individual therapist would. While the support group generally has a trained facilitator to lead the group, the facilitator's role is to keep everyone on track and to aid in the process of group support. If you feel as though you need to work through issues from your past rather than process what's happening to you right now, you may be best to start with counseling rather than a support group. You can always join a support group later.

What a support group can give you is the awareness that you

are not alone. When you sit down with a group of eight or ten individuals who have all experienced problems similar to your own, it helps you break down the feelings that you are to blame for what happened to you. You realize instead that your date is to blame and society is to blame for tolerating and promoting such hideous behavior.

A support group will also give you the opportunity to learn how to trust others. By trusting other women, you are more capable of trusting yourself. And if you're in a support group with men and women, it's an opportunity to relate to men and develop a mutual trusting relationship in a safe environment. One woman reported that her two-year involvement in a male/female support group was the catalyst for overcoming the effects of dating abuse.

Battered women's shelter

If you've been physically abused or have been threatened with abuse and are in need of protection, you may want to contact the closest battered women's shelter. Most shelters provide refuge to women who are married or living with their partners. This gets women (and children) out of the home which they share with the abuser. However, even if you aren't living with your abuser, if you fear that he will hurt you and being in your home feels dangerous, you need to consider a shelter.

Some women find that going to a friend's or relative's house serves the same purpose. If you feel safe doing this, then do so. One woman remembered how she sought help while in college. "Once, when I was again trying to break up with him, he gestured toward a flight of concrete stairs and growled, 'If you were a man, I'd bounce your head off of every step!' Another time, he called me when he was drunk and told me, 'I wanna lay you. I'm gonna do it, too.' I slept at a woman friend's house that night; and for weeks afterward, I was afraid to leave my room, even to go to class."

If you believe that instead of a friend's house, you need the safety and anonymity that a shelter provides, then make the call to get help.

In a battered women's shelter, besides food and a place to stay, you can expect help with prosecuting the abuser, finding other housing, counseling and support. In return, you'll be expected to follow certain house rules, such as not disclosing the location of the shelter and participating in household chores.

Because most women in the shelter are in spouse-like relationships and many have children by the man who's been abusing them, your dating relationship may appear simple in comparison. This is not to imply that you don't deserve and won't receive empathy. Rather, the other residents may question your need for safety when you aren't living with the abuser. You may also be told how lucky you are and how easy the situation is that you're in. I'm bringing this to your attention, not to discourage you from using a battered women's shelter but to prepare you for what you may encounter. And when you recognize that you're staying in a house with other women, some who've been married for many years and have several children, you can appreciate why your situation sounds "easy." Please don't take that to mean that you should ignore what's happened to you and continue dating the man who's been abusing you. Your emotional and physical wounds deserve as much care as anyone else's.

In a shelter, the crowded conditions mean that you are unlikely to get much privacy or reflective time. Shelters aren't like hotels with private rooms or private baths. Usually you share a room with other women and children. If you desperately need quiet space and can afford, it you may want to check into a motel.

Rape crisis center

If you've been date raped, then you should contact a rape crisis service. Some communities have an actual center where victims are treated medically and emotionally. Other places have a central hotline, and a trained volunteer or staff person will meet you in a hospital emergency room. However your community handles it, if you have a rape crisis service, you'll be assured of support and gentle care.

By seeking help after a date rape, you allow yourself to identify that you've been violated. Many women regret that they never sought help after a date rape because it kept them from truly believing that they were raped. Instead, they minimized it, blamed themselves, and sometimes pretended that it didn't happen. But it did happen. And being able to say that to yourself and to others is vital to healing.

The rape crisis service will help you receive appropriate medical attention. An advocate—another woman—can help you alleviate your fears and embarrassments during the medical examination. The examination is important to collect evidence (pubic hairs, semen, identification of injuries) should the case be heard in court. But even if you don't intend to prosecute, if you've been physically hurt, you need an exam.

Date rape and stranger rape differ. In a stranger rape, a woman should *always* seek medical care. Besides gathering evidence, the medical exam will also test for venereal disease or other related disorders such as pelvic inflammatory disease.

But in date rape, you know your assailant. If you've had consenting sex with him in the past, you assume that he doesn't have a venereal disease. And if he hasn't been violent or rough, you feel somewhat confident that there aren't any medical problems to attend to. What you're left with then are your emotions.

Date-rape survivors—after addressing any immediate medical concerns—need help in sorting out their emotions. A rape crisis service can give you this help also. The staff may provide anonymous telephone counseling which can give you the clarity you need to see the situation as rape. They may also have face-to-face counseling or provide support groups. It's important that you check out what's available and that you identify that it's date rape. Again be aware that women who've been raped by strangers may perceive your situation as easier than theirs. You don't have to wonder who did this to you or if he's secretly watching you. Because you know him and may have already dated him for awhile, your situation differs. But remember, you were physically raped as was the woman who was raped by a stranger. They are both manifestations of the same problem. You both deserve help in healing your wounds.

Police and prosecution

If you have been physically or sexually abused, you have the right to press charges against your assailant. Not a long-standing right of women, it's just in the past ten to fifteen years that women have gained strides in this area. But trying to prosecute an abuser is no easy task.

First, you must convince an official (usually a man) of the fact that a law has been broken. For some women, this has been a difficult, if not impossible, task.

Brenda, the woman who was nearly killed by Daryl—her "Dream Man", had little help from the police. After escaping from Daryl's apartment, Brenda said, "I was so terrified that he was coming after me, but he never did. I drove to the nearest shopping center and got out under a light to assess the damage. My scalp was bleeding, my eye was black, blood was coming through my blouse from where he had bitten me. My cheeks were bruised. There were numerous cuts on my face and arms from his fingernails, and I had a bruise the entire length of my upper thigh.

"I had to go by the police station on my way home, so I stopped there. Guess what they said?! I could not prove that I was invited in Daryl's house and since this happened at his place, he could say that I forced my way in and was trespassing. I couldn't believe my ears. They also said that since we weren't married, there was nothing they could do."

Daryl, whom she now refused to date, attempted to hurt Brenda later and once again the police were asked to intervene. "He was drunk and drove over to my apartment, standing outside waving a gun and threatening to finish the job he started. The police were not only called by myself, but my neighbors. The police told Daryl to go home and sleep it off and told me that Daryl was no danger to me since my apartment was on the second floor. They also inferred that I couldn't definitely see a gun from that far up.

"Daryl left long enough for the police to go and then returned. Again the neighbors called, and this time the police returned to see Daryl with gun in hand. They just told him to go home or they would have to give him a ticket for stopping the car in the middle of the street. I could not believe it."

What Brenda experienced with the police is not unusual—even in the 1980's. Unfortunately our society has allowed men to rape and beat women for so long that it's difficult for many to reframe their social thinking. Even when laws have been changed to protect women from abuse, the police are often slow to respond.

Other women indicated that college officials have basically been disinterested in intervening in what they view as "lovers' spats." One woman did report, however, that when the guy she was trying to break up with locked her in his apartment and raped her, he was expelled from college. But, he had already been reported for raping two other women on campus earlier in the year. This same woman also filed a report with the local police and nothing had been done by them.

One of the areas where the police and prosecutors can be beneficial is in securing restraining—or protective—orders. A restraining order is a court order which specifies that the abuser may not have contact with you. It can be written to forbid him from coming into your house, near your employment or making any type of contact with you whatsoever. If you want to secure a restraining order, you will most likely go to the district attorney's office and may be seen by a judge.

In some communities restraining orders are becoming more commonplace since many battered women seek them in order to protect themselves from their mate. But there are still problems in dealing with prosecutors and convincing them of the legitimacy of your request. One woman wrote of a man who had threatened to rape her and throw her down a flight of steps after she told him that she was breaking up with him. She suspected that he was following her because she'd see him in the parking lot near where she worked. She said, "I was really afraid of the guy and went to see a judge to see if I could get a protective order to keep him away from me. But, the judge brushed aside my concerns and just told me, 'Well, just don't go to places where y'all used to go, so you won't meet up with him.'"

Success at getting a restraining order, however, does not mean blanket protection. The restraining order simply means that if the guy violates the restrictions on the order, he will be in violation of the court and could stand prosecution for his actions. In other words, his behavior is no longer solely between the two of you; it's now between him and the judicial system.

Some men view a restraining order with respect and authority. It's enough to get them to stop the harassment and threats. Other men become more incensed when they receive the order and violate it in order to defy you and the courts.

So if you have a restraining order, keep it with you, be careful and be prepared to show it to the police if you need to contact them for a violation of the order. When they see that you have a court order against this guy, they'll take you and the situation more seriously.

Friends and family

Much of the support we receive for day-to-day living comes from family and friends. But in a dating-abuse situation, it's often difficult to rely on family and friends to see us through the pain.

Many women I spoke with told me that their family wasn't supportive. Marilyn, the woman whose boyfriend choked her in her college dorm, indicated that while in high school her boyfriend physically abused her in her own basement. Her screams for help resulted in her parents opening the door at the top of the stairs and yelling down that they should cut it out. That was the extent of her parents' involvement. Never did they ask her how she was or specifically what was happening. In fact, they even allowed this guy to live with them in their home during his last year of high school when he was kicked out of his parents' house.

Now in her 30s, what Marilyn resents most is her parents' lack of concern. Had they reached out to her, acknowledged that something harmful was happening or asked if she needed help, she may have had the support she needed to break up the relationship. Instead, it lasted for six years and nearly resulted in her death.

Dating-abuse survivors who were living at home during the time of the abuse particularly wanted to rely on their parents or siblings for support. For some women, they did have family who listened and believed them. One woman's father told her boyfriend to stop coming around after his daughter told him that she was afraid of the guy and he wouldn't leave her alone. Other women had sisters they could talk to and, in a sense, compare notes with.

A supportive family gives the dating-abuse survivor a solid base on which to assert herself. She has a backup system, a group of believers who will stick by her.

Likewise, friends can fulfill this role. When you have a friend who can help you check out your perceptions, it can help you feel more confident in your judgment. It can also serve to minimize self-blame. Naturally a friend who defends the guy, insists that you must have done something to provoke him, and berates you for your poor choice in dates, is hardly the type of friend you're looking for at this time.

If you don't feel that you can get the understanding and support you need from your family or friends, seek other help. You should not be left alone with your confused feelings.

New Partner

When it comes time to date someone new and to establish another dating relationship, your new partner can be a source of support.

Many women told me of new relationships and how they had communicated and incorporated what had happened to them into those relationships. One woman spoke of her new partner—now her husband—as the provider of outside validation that she had been missing. Coming from an emotionally neglectful family and settling for dates who'd eventually abuse her, this woman gained little esteem from the men she had dated. Somehow through it all, she met the man she'd marry and marveled at this caring, thoughtful, sensitive man who wanted to spend his life with her. When she shared her past and how she'd been abused, he accepted it as a part of her.

For other women, however, the process is slower. Marilyn, the woman who dated an abuser for six years while her parents ignored the situation, had flashbacks and nightmares which haunted her for seven years after the relationship ended. When she began to develop a dating relationship with Jim, the man she eventually married, she'd often get anxiety attacks. Once when she and Jim were putting up a Christmas tree, she fled the room when Jim's anger grew at the uncooperative tree stand. Other times, she'd freeze, tense up and tell him to move away from her when, objectively, the situation was not threatening. But *subjectively* it was. For Marilyn, she needed to learn to trust a man. The guy who abused her was her first boyfriend, and her husband Jim was the first man she developed an intimate, on-going relationship with since she got out of the abusive one.

Vital to the continuing of their relationship was Marilyn's disclosure to Jim of what she'd been through. With that information, he could develop understanding and empathy for her feelings.

In order to get support from your new partner, you need to let him in. Share what's comfortable for you right now. Don't disclose more than you feel ready to disclose. Take the pace of the relationship as it comes. If you keep your partner out of your past and the abuses you've suffered, you're not being fair to yourself or to him.

This is not to guarantee closeness or understanding on his part. In fact, you are taking a risk. One woman told her partner of a date rape and was accused of provoking it herself. Clearly, if your new partner responds as this man did, you may find that you have another insensitive man in your life.

For some women, developing a new, lasting relationship may indicate the need to go into therapy together. Often the pains of dating abuse are too tender and too deep to disclose on your own. A caring, sensitive partner will listen to your need to work out issues in a trusting, safe environment. It's an option you may want to explore.

A new partner must realize that he's coming into this relationship while you may have some old baggage laying around. Your life is filled with real fears and irrational ones. As you begin to trust your new partner, hopefully the real fears will dissipate. If they don't, you're in another potentially abusive situation. But the irrational fears may linger. They stay around much longer because your subconscious attempts to protect you. So the messages that you'll be left, hurt, deceived or abused creep into your life. These messages can damage a good relationship if they aren't resolved. But if you can both understand where they come from, how they surface, and how to handle it, then your new relationship has the potential to grow in a healthy manner.

Part Four

Prevention

18

Ten Warning Signs

Although dating abuse can surface at a moment's notice without any prior warning, many times there are sufficient signals which indicate impending abuse. In the past, women didn't recognize the danger signs because they didn't know that they existed. Only much later, after they'd already been abused, did they go back over the relationship—however short or long in duration—and realize that there were clues which they could have picked up on to avoid being abused.

This list of warning signs is compiled from the hundreds who responded to my request for information. These are the behaviors they later recognized as the warning signs of abuse. Dating-abuse survivors want you to know about them so that you too can be forewarned.

1. Bad vibes

The first and foremost warning sign begins with yourself. When you sense that something isn't right with the relationship, it's a sign that you could be hurt emotionally or physically.

You feel crummy. You're scared. You think that you might get hurt. You feel as though you're losing a part of yourself. You seem to be a chameleon, always changing in order to please your date.

When your intuition says that something's wrong, trust it. If you can identify what's wrong with the relationship, you may be able to change it. If the problem is that you fail to be yourself, start being you. Say what you want to say. If you normally go along with his decisions on where to go, indicate that you don't want to see a certain movie if that's what you're feeling. Be yourself and trust yourself.

And if the issue seems to be with your date, do you feel comfortable sharing your concerns? If you don't, that's a clue that you're in a dangerous situation. If you can't tell him that what he said or did scares you, what does that mean about who's in control of the relationship? And if you've just met this guy, don't go anywhere alone with him under these circumstances. If you can tell your date your feelings and concerns, do it.

Frame your comments with "I" Statements.

- I'm feeling scared right now.
- I don't want to go to a movie tonight.
- I don't want to get sexual just now.
- I'm ready to go home.

When you use "I" Statements, you're talking about *you*, not him, and you lessen the possibility for your date to get defensive. But if your date discounts your concerns or gets overly defensive, take that as another warning signal. What's he really telling you? That he doesn't want to hear about your feelings? That he's more concerned with himself than with you?

Your intuition is your sense of what's right and wrong. Sometimes it's just a vague feeling. You can't pin it down. You don't quite know what the problem is. Many women indicated to me that they later wished they had acted on their vague feelings.

Trust the feelings. If it feels like the relationship isn't good for you, it's not good for you. Don't excuse him. Don't blame yourself.

Learning to trust yourself and your feelings is the first step in avoiding an abusive relationship. It's what you rely on to refuse that first date or to end a long-standing relationship. It's also what you use to make changes in order to build a healthy relationship.

2. Aggression

If you put aggression on a continuum, you'll find that on the one end there's perhaps a temper flare-up while on the other end, there's physical violence which could result in death. Because aggression has the potential to be life-threatening, none of it should be taken lightly.

Everyone gets angry. It's a universal emotion. But it's what your date does with his anger that determines whether he's an aggressive person.

A person who routinely cannot handle normal daily frustrations without shouting, cursing and pounding fists is someone who has difficulty handling angry feelings. Be concerned about your date if he treats animals cruelly, has a fascination with weapons or screams at you instead of talking things out.

If your date shows signs of physical aggression: grabbing you by the arm, punching you, slapping you in the face, hitting or biting, you already know that he's a physical abuser. These signals mean that more is yet to come. Enough is already known about men who abuse women to indicate that once abuse begins, it continues. Sometimes a man can get help for his problem, go to a special program for batterers and learn to control his aggression. But even then, he must spend time unlearning a long-held behavioral pattern. For someone with an aggression problem, it's easier to be aggressive than to be non-aggressive. It takes a man with a huge personal conviction to commit himself to change his violent habits. Even then, it requires outside help through counseling or self-help groups.

If you find out that your date has abused other women, heed the warning. Many women fail to trust the other women, former dating partners or wives, and instead make excuses for the man they're dating. They infer that the other women provoked the abuse. But the circumstances of other women's abuse aren't necessarily important. What's important is that other women were abused by *your* date. This means that your date abuses women. You are a woman. You are vulnerable to abuse.

One survivor's advice: "If the guy offers physical violence even once—drop him! Don't take the chance that when he promises, 'I'll never do it again,' he'll be the one-in-a-million that won't. Life is too short."

3. Jealousy

One of the most consistent behaviors and attitudes of abusive men is jealousy. As we've seen in the accounts cited in this book, jealousy can be an extremely damaging element in a dating relationship.

Some signs of jealousy include

- accusing you of dating or flirting with someone else when you've done no such thing;
- getting excessively angry if you talk to another guy;
- questioning you harshly about where you were, who you were with, and what you were wearing; and
- not believing you when you respond to his accusations.

If you're questioned this way and have nothing to feel guilty about—yet you do feel guilty, it's a good sign that your partner is the jealous type. A jealous man has a knack for turning things around and blaming the woman for his outrage and anger. As with physical aggression, jealousy continues, not lessens, with the length of the relationship. It will only get worse the more involved you are with this guy. And to make the situation even more complex, the jealous man will lead you into believing that marriage and a long-term commitment will change him into becoming more secure.

Don't believe him. The jealous man has a self-esteem problem and he's trying to compensate for it through you. You have a choice to make as to whether or not you'll let him do it. Jealousy is not love. It's control.

One dating-abuse survivor warned, "A man who sulks or tries to pressure you when you say, 'Sorry, I need to study' or 'I can't go with you because Sue and I agreed to go out that night' is manipulative. He should stop it after you point it out to him a few times, at the most. If he doesn't, *Watch Out!* This type often winds up accusing you of having sex with every man you say 'Hello' to."

4. Controlling behaviors

Men control women because women let them. Often subtle, some men tell their dates how to dress, what to say, and who they can associate with. One woman reported that the guy she dated always asked her out on Wednesday nights, the one night when she had standing plans with a woman friend to play tennis. Try as he might to coerce her in giving up her plans—and her friend—this woman refused to be pressured.

Other women, however, aren't as quick to pick up on controlling behaviors. Not until the relationship has deteriorated into his power and her submission does the woman realize that she's lost contact with all of her old friends and activities. This type of control leads to isolation. And isolation leads to vulnerability for abuse.

If you feel as though you are losing yourself because of your date, you may be coming under his control. Is he insisting that you do things you don't agree with?

When you determine for yourself not to let this happen, you have the power to change it. You may merely need to be more self-assertive and believe in yourself. Or, if your date refuses to *allow* you to make your own decisions, see your own friends and participate in your own activities, it's time to reconsider the relationship. No guy is worth losing control over your own life.

5. Misogyny

Misogyny, or the hatred of all women, is an unperceived element in many dating abuse situations because most women are unaware of the underlying meaning involved in what misogynist men say and do.

Sexist remarks and denigrating comments about women indicate that a man is incapable of a relationship based on mutual respect.

Examples may include

- "You're smart—for a woman." Thrown out as a supposed compliment, it really means that this guy considers women less intelligent than men.
- "Did you see those women down at the music festival. The way they're dressed, they're just asking to be raped." A belief that women are responsible for being raped may mean that he's raped women, or certainly that if you were raped he'd consider it your fault.

- "A woman could never run for President. They're too dizzy." Again, men are better than women; therefore, he's better than you.
- "The reason that women aren't better at math and science is because they aren't capable of such technical matters." If he won't hear your rationale that women aren't encouraged to excel in these areas and are discriminated against, be careful.
- "I don't think that a guy should have to work for a woman boss." Is he implying that it's beneath a man to work for someone *inferior*? Or that women are too *emotional*? Or too *flighty*? Check it out.
- "All women use men." This is a man who's angry at women he's been involved with. He's setting you up so you'll be extra nice to him and not be like "all women." In reality, you can't win because he'll find a way to believe that you used him too.
- "Women are spoiled. They always want everything their own way." The message here is "Do it my way." How can you assert your rights with a guy who translates that into being "spoiled?"
- "Figures! A woman driver." Don't men drivers make mistakes?

When misogynists go unchecked, as they often do, they continue to add to their belief system that males are superior. This promotes an underlying sexism and hatred towards women. Referring to women as "broads," "dames," "pieces of ass," or "prick teasers" and to parts of women's anatomy as "knockers," "cunt," "slit," or" pussy" promotes women as objects to be used by men. Stay clear of guys who don't respect women as their equals, and especially be wary of those who degrade all women with their words and actions. Remember, he's really telling you what he thinks of *you*.

6. Put downs

In the same way, let a warning flag go up when you are personally put down. If a guy puts you down on the first date, it's a clear sign that he's a verbal abuser.

The first date, the time when you want to show your best side, should not include comments about how horribly you're dressed, how dumb or clumsy you are, or how flawed your personality is. You can be sure that if you're deflated on this first date, only bad times are to follow.

But a date who gets past the first or several dates without demeaning you, may start it later on. Always having to be right, needing to win at games, attacking your intelligence for losing, or if he doesn't win, finding a way to minimize the fact that you did are signs of his poor self-image. He needs to make you look bad so that he'll feel better.

Other men go to the extremes of demeaning their date with comments like,

"You're nothing but a whore."

"Who else would want to date you; you're lucky to have me."

"Hey, Fatty!"

"Get over here, you cunt."

"Good thing you're a woman, 'cause you'd never get a good enough job to support a family if you were a man."

If you want the put downs to stop, make it clear that they won't be tolerated. Remember, you can't make him stop what he's doing, you can only tell him that you don't like it and won't tolerate it. He has to stop it on his own or with outside help. If he keeps it up and won't get counseling to deal with his self-esteem problems, get out of the relationship before he takes your self-esteem down to his level.

7. Pornography

Enough studies have been done to determine that men who engage in excessive pornographic activities have lower opinions of women and are more likely to view women as sexual objects. They are also more likely to sexually abuse a woman than men who don't read porn magazines or go to pornographic films.

Because so much of pornography depicts women as unequal or as victims, it promotes the myths that women want to be raped or to be treated rough. True erotica, the depiction of men and women as equal, romantic players, is a rare commodity in our society.

If the guy you're dating has stacks of pornographic magazines, ask him why he has them. If he watches porn movies, find out what he enjoys about them. If he wants you to watch them with him, be prepared to see women in demeaning, uncompromising and violent experiences.

You may be able to talk to your date about your concerns and convince him that his pastime is less than honorable. But if it concerns you a lot, is acted out in his behavior towards you, and he won't change his reading or viewing habits, you'd best reconsider your safety in this relationship.

8. Unpleasant sex

Sex which is hurtful or unpleasant is a warning sign of worse things to come. Demands to perform sex acts against your wishes, rough sex, sex which is painful, or coercive tricks to get you to have sex are indications of what this guy will continue to expect from you.

Again, trust yourself. If something doesn't feel right, act on it. If you meet a man at a party and pick up signs that this guy is too rough for you, don't go anywhere with him alone. If you're in an ongoing relationship, speak up if you feel safe doing so. He'll either stop, continue, or get worse. If he stops, talk it out. Explain how you feel. Use "I" Statements.

- I was scared.
- It didn't feel good to me.
- That was too rough for me.

If he continues despite your pleas or gets worse, then you clearly have a sign that this is what to expect if you stay involved with this guy.

9. Drinking and drugs

Although drinking and drugs do not mean that a man will become abusive, many women report that their abusers were involved with alcohol or drugs. Some women subsequently refuse to date guys who drink or take drugs.

If you just meet someone and he gets drunk, don't go anywhere alone with him. You don't know him and can't gauge his drunken behavior, much less his sober behavior. Also, if you've never seen your date drunk before, be careful about being alone with him if he does get inebriated. At the first signs of abusive behavior—put downs, aggression, unfounded jealousy—get away to a safe place. Don't leave yourself open to being vulnerable.

Monitor your own drinking and drug usage with someone you've just met. Keep your head clear so that you can assess the situation and keep tabs on warning signs. Drugs and alcohol will only cloud your thinking.

10. Childhood violence

If your date comes from a family in which there was violence—child abuse, wife beating—he may be prone to follow the example and abuse you too. Rarely does this topic surface on the first date, however. But it is something you should bring up when the timing seems appropriate. As you talk about his past, if abuse was a part of his family life, ask him how he coped. How does it affect him now? What does he think about corporal punishment for children? Does a man have the right to hit his wife? Answers to these questions will give you clues on how he may behave with you.

Similarly, your own background of childhood violence could lead you into believing that you deserve to be mistreated. Be honest with yourself and accept this as your personal warning sign that you are a vulnerable woman. Get help and counseling to overcome your feelings of inadequacy. You are a special person who deserves to be treated decently. No one has the right to abuse another person. No one has the right to mistreat you.

These warning signs give you clues to help determine whether you're in a potentially abusive relationship. Although not definitive, they should help you recognize what is unhealthy about your relationship. Particularly when you are starting a new relationship, these ten warning signs can give you a checklist to determine what to be wary of. Use it to assist you in making wise and healthy choices.

And remember—*trust your instincts.*

19

An Ounce of Prevention

Heeding the warning signs of possible abuse is the beginning of preventing abuse. But there are also other pro-active steps you can take. When you focus solely on warning signs, you take all of your cues from your date. He acts; you react. And while this is vitally important, it shouldn't be the only thing you do.

Establishing your own preventive measures will help you control the outcome of the date rather than surrendering control to the guy you're with. These suggestions have been tried by other dating women. Use what's meaningful to you and add your own to the list.

Be able to leave.

Many women now take their own cars to meet a date at a designated location. This gives you a chance to get to know him better before giving him your home address. It also means that you are under no obligation to get into his car, a potentially vulnerable place to be. If you choose to go somewhere with him in his car, it's exactly that—a choice.

If you don't have your own car, do what mothers have been telling their daughters to do for decades. Carry money for a phone call. And use it if you need someone to come and give you a ride home. Also, carry bus or cab money.

Plan for the chance that you may need or want to make your own way home. This can occur because it's been a boring evening, unpleasant, uncomfortable or threatening. Don't be caught off guard with no means of transporting yourself and stuck with getting into his car. You have the right to get home safely. Don't worry about seeming rude. If he's a caring, sensitive man, he'll understand your caution and be impressed with your ability to take care of yourself. And if he's put off with your desire to transport yourself, he's probably not worth any more of your time.

Pay your own way.

More and more women are feeling comfortable paying their own way on dates, particularly the first few. You don't know him; he doesn't know you. So why should you be obligated to him?

For many women, paying their own way when they go out with a man is the same as paying their own way when they go out with their women friends. Would you expect your good friend Elaine to treat you every time the two of you went out together? Of course not.

If you can get your comfort level up to the point of paying your own way, you'll feel more in control of the situation. You won't have to feel that you're responsible for making sure that he's having a good time. You won't feel that you owe him something in return. Don't forget the belief that "I spent good money on you, now you owe me sex" still lives. Paying your own way is a way to break the cycle.

Suppose you tell your date that you intend to pay your own way—and he's insulted. What does that mean about the guy you're going out with? Is he just old-fashioned? Or is he threatened by the equality you're establishing in the relationship from the start?

Because you pay your own way doesn't mean that you're taking the romance out of dating. We've already disputed the myth of being swept off our feet. Rather it gives you a chance to establish an equitable, no-strings-attached relationship so that later, when your date says he wants to treat you to dinner and a concert, it's special, not assumed.

Decrease interaction time.

If the situation with your date, or the guy you just met at a bar or party, becomes uncomfortable, don't continue to spend time with him. Too often, some guy tries to get overly friendly, and even though we think he's a jerk, we continue to make conversation with him. You don't have an obligation to entertain him.

Practice saying, "Excuse me, but I need to talk to a friend of mine over there." Then, don't wait for a response, just go. Even if you don't know someone "over there," you can walk up to a woman and start talking. Any woman will understand when you explain to her that you're getting away from some guy who's been annoying you.

When you continue to talk with a guy you're not interested in, you inadvertently encourage his paying attention to you. If you don't want his attention, remove yourself from his proximity.

Decreasing interaction time means trusting your instincts. Something's not right. You feel scared. You're threatened. You have an overwhelming urge to run away. Act on your feelings.

If you're with a date in his apartment, know where to go in order to escape should the situation turn threatening. Because most women feel a sense of trust for the man they're with, they don't think about escape routes. After all, you wouldn't willfully be alone in an apartment with a man you thought might rape you. Make a habit then of scanning any new place for a way out regardless of imminent threat. Think about it in terms of a fire, if you must. How would you get out? Does the bathroom lock and is there a window to scream for help? Is there one exit or more? Is there a lock on it and how does it work? Any information you can glean while the situation appears safe will aid you tremendously should an emergency arise.

The sooner you can leave a private, enclosed location when you sense danger, the safer you'll be. Don't worry about appearing rude. Your safety is of greater concern. Trusting those instincts will keep you safe.

Assert Yourself.

If you're having trouble getting someone away from you, tell the guy point blank that you aren't interested.

"I want you to leave me alone now."

"I don't care to talk to you."

"I'm going to call the manager if you don't get away from me."

Going this route will mean that you or someone you're with should keep an eye out for where this guy goes. Don't walk to your car alone and watch to see if you are being followed home.

When a situation like this happened to me in a restaurant of a shopping mall, I loudly told the man, "Stop bothering us. Leave us alone!" Immediately I called the restaurant manager who contacted the mall security. The man who was bothering my woman friend and me had also harassed and threatened other women that evening. While the head of security was looking for the guy throughout the mall, another guard escorted my friend and me to our respective cars.

In the past, women haven't wanted to "create a scene" over a guy who's bothering them. But even if it's the guy you came with, why protect *him* from embarrassment if he's threatening *you*? Women must stop allowing potential abusers—particularly date rapists—to hide. If he's bothering you, he'll bother some other woman too. Imagine if all of the women a man had harassed or threatened in one evening, or one week, or one month, or one year, got together and told him that they expected it to stop. It would be a mighty powerful scene.

When you use assertion as a preventive tool, it puts you back in control. It may or may not change what's happening, but at least you've said what you're thinking and feeling. One woman told me of a mild case of date abuse which she refused to submit to. She and her date had gone to a play which she considered to have heavy sexist overtones. When she told her date at intermission that she thought the play was pretty awful, he proceeded to tell her that she wasn't enjoying it because the brand of humor was obviously too sophisticated for her. She said, "From then on it was a series of criticisms of everything I had to say."

Eventually she told him, "Look, it seems I can't say anything right tonight. I think maybe I'd better go. It was nice of you to invite me, and I'm sorry I didn't enjoy the play. Good night." Then she walked out.

She considered this experience as, "A non-event, an unspeakably mild case of abuse thwarted, but a victory for me in my struggle for self-respect and the respect of others. Two years ago, I would have silently submitted to his put downs and gone home—possibly with him—wondering how I could improve myself so I could win his approval."

Learning to become assertive can be a difficult task. Women are trained to be passive and submissive, and even more so when it comes to a relationship with a man. If you have the chance to take a class in assertiveness training, give it a try. Or call your nearest women's center and ask if they would offer one. But don't let the unavailability of formal training keep you from learning the basic assertive skills. Get a book from your library or bookstore and practice either with a friend or alone in front of a mirror. Soon you'll develop confidence that you can say what you really think and feel in a way that seems right for you and doesn't demean others.

Getting to know him

One woman, abused by several of her former dates, developed criteria to determine the men she wanted to date or continue dating. She decided that she wanted someone who respected her as a person, who treated women as equals, and who shared an equal responsibility for the success of the relationship.

After initially meeting a man and trusting her intuition that she'd like to spend time getting to know him, she'd accept a date with him. Then on the first or several dates she'd start conversations which would give her the answers to her questions.

- How did he feel about the Feminist Movement?
- What were his thoughts about birth control—whose responsibility should it be, the man's or woman's?

Answers to these and other questions gave her a measure against which to judge the men she wanted to avoid. By doing so, she prevented any subsequent abusive dating relationships. And she eventually met and married her husband—who met all of her criteria.

In developing your own criteria of the type of man you want, remember to include your parameter of decent treatment—what you expect and don't expect out of a dating relationship. Review "The Dating Woman's Bill of Rights" regularly. Say it aloud often and believe it. Make a pact with yourself that you deserve decent treatment and you will not continue to date someone who abuses you.

If a first date does not fall within the parameters you've set for yourself, ask yourself why you'd want to date this guy again. If you do decide to continue dating him to give him a chance, make it clear to him early on that there are certain things you will not tolerate in a relationship. If he can't respect this now, he won't later on. One woman who was abused in a past relationship told her new date up front that she wouldn't tolerate any physical abuse. She was less fearful and felt more in control after making this statement.

Getting to know who you are dating means finding out what he's like as a person and how he treats women. Ask him questions about his own family background. Does he have sisters? How is his relationship with them? What does he say about his mother? Was there violence in his childhood? Was he abused as a kid? Did his father abuse his mother? Were there alcohol or drug problems in his family? How did his family deal with anger? How does he feel about these things now?

Clearly you won't pull out this book, turn to this page, and drill your date on these questions *per se*. Instead, ask the questions you're comfortable with in an exchange of dialogue about both your families' backgrounds. His responses to your information are also clues as to how he'll relate to you later on. If he's only interested in talking about himself, he'll hardly be there for you when you need him.

When you piece together the picture of your current perception of who he is with what he tells you about his past, you'll be better prepared to assess whether this is a relationship you want to pursue or a guy you want to avoid.

By determining who to avoid, women are more aware of who to attract. So often women date men just because the men ask. It's not because there's any real attraction or connection. It's not because their philosophies are in sync or because they share so much in common. Dating someone just because they ask creates a vulnerability to abuse. One woman even identified that all of the men who abused her over the years came from that category. When she dated men because she wanted to date them, she wasn't abused. Being able to refuse dates with men you don't want to go out with means that you're accepting the notion that you don't need a man— just any man—in order to fulfill yourself.

Keep your friends.

No matter how wonderful and non-abusive your date may be, it's important to keep your own friends. When you give away your contact with other people—except your date and his friends—your social life is dependent entirely on him. After awhile your dependence on him is so great that you don't even consider breaking up with him even if he is abusive.

Keeping your own friends gives you several important elements to consider when you're dating someone.

First, you have other things to do besides go out on a date. This serves to remind your date that you are a person in your own right who existed before he came into your life and who will exist long after he leaves your life.

Second, your friends are the people you can lean on if times get rough. They can give you support, cheer you up, and see you through it all.

Third, your friends can give you feedback about your date. What do they think about him? How do they perceive how he treats you? Do they think you and he are a good match? If your friends, who have known you longer than your date has are telling you negative things about this relationship, trust what they're saying then check it out with your own underlying feelings.

If you give up your own friends you have no one to depend on but your date. *Dependency* means *vulnerability*. *Vulnerability* leads to *abuse*.

Preventing date rape

A date rapist can be slick. He works on harboring your trust then turns on you when you least expect it. We've seen throughout this book that many women were date raped under unassuming circumstances.

But date rape can often be prevented by being alert and attentive to warning signs and by following preventive measures in avoiding date-rape attempts. If you find yourself in a situation which is vulnerable to date rape, the first thing you need to do is get out.

At the first sign that your date isn't respecting your desire not to be amorous, leave. Don't give him any room to misjudge your intentions. Get up, remove yourself from his presence, and leave. You don't need to talk about it or explain your actions with anything more than, "I'm leaving." You can always give him more feedback later if you care to. And definitely don't date this guy again unless you talk it out with him and he clearly understands what you're telling him. Even then, be cautious in where you go with him until you can trust that he won't coerce or force you into having sex.

If you aren't able to get up to leave, assert yourself. Saying things like, "Stop doing that!" "Don't touch me!" "You're hurting me. Stop it!" give him a clear and firm message that you don't like what he's doing and you expect it to stop. If he continues you may have to threaten to report him for sexual assault or rape. An assertive woman can verbally disarm a date rapist who is basically looking for a passive and indecisive victim.

One woman, who was being pushed down onto a bed by her date, kept sitting herself up and telling her date, "No! I don't want to have sex with you." Finally tired of trying to get her to give in, he let go of her shoulders and she bolted for the door. Resisting at the first signs of dominance and control can prevent the rape from ever taking place.

Yelling can also be an effective preventive tool to ward off the date rapist who wants his pastime to remain anonymous. If you can blow his cover and create a scene, it may shock him enough to leave you alone. If you're in a car, try to honk the horn. Anywhere yell and scream, "Help! He's raping me!" If you yell and throw things around at the same time, your crazed behavior may create enough of a shock effect to allow you to escape injury.

Trickery is another form of date-rape prevention that many women have succeeded in using. Some women have used trickery when they were sure that they were going to be date raped. Other women used trickery to get away after a date rape had occurred and the rapist still wouldn't let her go. Saying that a friend was waiting and would be looking for her, agreeing to date the guy again, or offering to get him a drink of water are all excuses women have used to get away so that they wouldn't be raped repeatedly. Prepare yourself by becoming familiar with rape prevention techniques. A good resource is *Fear or Freedom* by Susan E. Smith, published by Mother Courage Press.

If you are date raped even after heeding the warning signs and practicing preventive measures, be assured that it wasn't your fault. Prevention can dissipate some potential abuse; but it can never prevent it all. If you continue to be abused even after using these techniques, he's to blame, not you. Trust yourself that you did your best to avoid it and that, in this instance, it was unavoidable. And if you see a warning sign in retrospect, use it in the *future* to protect you—not in the *present to blame yourself.*

Trust yourself.

There's no clearer preventive tool than to trust yourself explicitly. You are the person who knows what is right for you and you are the judge of what is good for you. Getting to know, like and trust yourself is the best prevention you can have.

If you've had a series of abusive dating relationships, you probably doubt your ability to pick a non-abusing date. So trust that feeling and use it to learn more about what attracts you to abusive men.

- Do you think that you don't deserve better?
- Were you abused as child and expect that those who care about you will abuse you too?
- Do you confuse abuse with love?

Whatever your underlying belief system, you can change it to "The Dating Woman's Bill of Rights."

Believing in yourself and your right not to be abused in a relationship allows you to rely on your feelings and intuition. You know when something isn't right. Trusting yourself means that you'll act on your feelings more often. You'll be able to check things out, avoid unpleasant and potentially harmful situations and get out of relationships that hurt you. You won't need an overwhelming amount of evidence before you act. You won't wait until he nearly kills you or rapes you if you trust your early feelings that he's a threat to you.

Trust in yourself is your ticket to taking care of yourself. And when you take care of yourself, you refuse to let anyone abuse you.

20

Healthy Responses to Dating-Abuse Situations

Heeding the warning signs and following preventive measures will minimize the extent of abuse you'll suffer in dating situations. But it can't eliminate it entirely. Even when you succeed in thwarting a full-blown case of date abuse, you'll still be dealing with the elements that caused you to switch into preventive gear. And there will be times when abuse occurs without warning or time for you to respond. So when abusive dating situations occur, how are you to respond?

Assess the wounds.

How were you hurt? Is the pain solely emotional or are there physical damages? Do you require medical care?

Many women fail to take proper assessment of their well-being following dating abuse. Instead they minimize what happened, often denying date rape or physical assault. It's difficult to admit that your date—particularly if it's someone you trust—could have hurt you this way. It seems easier to ignore it, to avoid the realities of the wounds and pretend that it never happened. But ignoring the wounds only adds to greater long-standing pain.

Whatever level of dating abuse, an objective assessment followed by a subjective review of your feelings will give you a head start in healing.

First, identify what happened. Were you physically abused? Sexually assaulted? Verbally put down?

Second, assess the damages. Are you cut, bruised or bleeding? What kind of pain are you in? Physical as well as emotional? Are you frightened?

Take action.

Don't become part of the conspiracy of silence. If you need medical assistance, get it. Seek support for yourself so you don't feel isolated. Remember, it's happening to other women too.

We've seen that support can come from friends, family, counselors and other women who've been abused. Find support which feels the best to you and seek it out.

If you need a period of social withdrawal in order to inner reflect, take that time. But don't ignore the need to share what's happened with others. For many of the women who contacted me, I was the first person they shared their story with. They feared ridicule, embarrassment, doubt and admonishment if they told anyone. So they kept it inside until I asked for them to be heard.

You don't have to keep the pain inside for years as so many others have. Seeking support allows you to unload the pain and gives you room to rebuild yourself.

Put the blame where it belongs.

No matter what occurs, do not blame yourself with "If onlys."
- If only I hadn't gone to his apartment with him.
- If only I had stayed at the party.
- If only I had acted on that warning sign sooner.
- If only I hadn't said that to him.

Promise yourself that you will put responsibility where it belongs—with the abuser. Don't blame it on the circumstances or the use of drugs or alcohol. Your date made a choice when he abused you. He decided to abuse you. It was his choice and his abuse of you. He didn't have to do it, but he did. He is to blame, not you.

Putting the blame where it belongs frees you to deal with your other emotions. It allows you to let the hurt, pain, sadness or anger surface. When you admit that someone abused you, then you refuse to accept that somehow you did this to yourself. It lets you view what happened to you so that you can take action.

Admit you made a mistake.

Admitting that you made a mistake which resulted in getting abused isn't the same as taking the blame for being abused. It means instead that you made an error, not that you caused yourself to be abused.

A 41-year-old Tacoma, Washington, woman who was date raped twice said, "At least I felt that the men, not me, had the severe problems. I was in the wrong places at the wrong times with the wrong people. I enjoy men who treat me well. I have had some wonderful dates in my life."

This woman is able to take the situations she's endured and put them into a healthier framework. She's not berating herself for what she did wrong. Yet, she's willing to admit that she was in the wrong place, that it was the wrong time, and she was with the wrong people. By giving herself the ability to acknowledge that mistakes were made, she's also realizing that she has control over her destiny. Next time, she may recognize that wrong place, time, or person before the abuse occurs.

If you can't admit a mistake, then you'll leave your dating fate to chance. You assume that you have no control over whom you date and what happens on a date.

The ability to admit a mistake doesn't mean that you make mistakes in every dating-abuse situation. Rather, it allows you to review what happened to see if there was something you did which made you vulnerable to abuse. When you're aware of the potential for making mistakes and you look for what they could be, you give yourself the gift of learning what you could avoid or change in the future.

Face your own problems.

Although the man who abused you is responsible for what he did to you, it doesn't mean that you are problem-free. The ability to face your own problems will give you an edge in your decisions about dating relationships.

- Are you a woman who always seems to get abused by her dates?
- Do the guys who abuse you have similar characteristics?
- Do you wonder why you're attracted to guys who abuse you?

Finding the pieces that you have control over will give you just that—control over your choice of dates. When you face the problems you bring into your dating relationships, it doesn't mean that you're blaming yourself for being abused. And correcting the problems also doesn't mean that you won't be abused anymore. But it's a way for you to understand that your underlying problems are issues which you can resolve. And when resolved, you'll be in a stronger position to avoid abuse or deal with it if it occurs again.

Also, facing any of your problems, even those unrelated to dating abuse, will help to make you a stronger person.

Seek justice.

Following through on prosecution of a date rape or physical assault gives you a feeling of control over what's occurred. It's a means for you to regain a sense of power in what was otherwise a powerless experience.

For women who don't prosecute, there's often a longer period of recovery from the emotional and psychological effects of dating abuse. Prosecution means that you're willing to admit that you were abused and willing to demand that justice be served. Justice, on the other hand, may or may not be served in your case. The man may never spend a minute in jail. But he'll know that he broke the law, that he got caught, that his name is registered on a complaint. And it will also mean that should he assault another woman who files a complaint against him, your prior complaint will give weight to hers.

If the situation doesn't warrant prosecution, tell someone—a friend, relative or other trusted person—about what happened. You need the feedback from another person.

Also, don't overlook the possibility of speaking up to your date who abused you. Before you do it though, get in touch with your inner feelings. If you're overwhelmed by fear, you may not feel safe talking to him. But if you do feel safe, tell your date that what he did hurt you. Be specific and use "I" Statements.

- I was raped by you last night. I'm very hurt, both physically and emotionally. I don't ever want to see you again.
- I was abused when you slapped me. I won't tolerate this.
- I felt hurt that you didn't show up for our date. And I was also worried that something happened to you.
- I felt demeaned by your comment about my weight. It's a sensitive subject for me. I need to be with a guy who supports me—not someone who puts me down.

Seeking justice, therefore, can come about through the court system or through your own system. Note that I'm not talking about *revenge*. Revenge puts you on his level and there's no need to compromise yourself. Justice allows you to feel that you've been honest and straightforward. You're asserting your rights not to be abused and you're regaining a part of you which your date attempted to destroy—your self-esteem.

21

Elements of a Healthy Relationship

An awareness of the elements of a healthy relationship will help you to recognize when a relationship is unhealthy. Many women don't know that relationships can be free from abuse, believing instead that all relationships harbor some abusive aspects. Undeniably, there is no such thing as a perfect, one hundred percent harmonious relationship. Because a dating relationship involves two people with feelings and emotions, there will be times when the partners are angry, hurt or defensive. But even these more negative aspects don't have to lead to abuse. When the relationship is a healthy one, the problems and issues can be worked through without annihilating either partner in the process.

Think about each one of these six elements needed in a healthy relationship and relate your current—or your next—dating relationship to each element.

Ask yourself

- Do we have mutual respect for one another?
- Do we trust each other?
- Is sex mutually enjoyable?
- Are we supportive of each other?
- Do we fight fair?
- Are we relaxed with each other?

Respect

In a dating relationship, mutual respect means that you each care about the other person while you also care about yourself. This is manifested through respecting the other's decisions or choices and listening to your partner's explanation of why those decisions were made.

With mutual respect, there's no room for put downs, snide remarks or denigrations. You both recognize that you can't change the other person. You can't force another person to be someone you want that person to be. What you can do, however, is let that person know who you are, what your needs are, and what you want from him and the relationship.

In a healthy relationship, if your date changes as a result of what you've shared, you don't gloat over believing that you changed him. You didn't. He changed himself because he wanted to change. This is an important distinction to make because in an unhealthy relationship, one partner often changes the behavior because of being manipulated, coerced or threatened. We've seen how this can occur in many dating-abuse situations. The changes, therefore, in unhealthy relationships, such as dress style, giving into sexual demands or choice of friends, occur not from an inner drive to change but from external pressures to do so.

In a healthy relationship, you must believe and respect that you can't change your partner. But if there are things you'd like *him* to change, be willing to share your feelings and needs with him. Give him the opportunity to change. If you find yourself demanding a change, check to see if this is because what you need changed is abusive to you. If it is, and he won't change it, you're in an unhealthy relationship.

Trust

A healthy relationship is built on trust. Devoid of lies, manipulations and secrets, there's a sense of companionship and caring.

Jealousy, the enigma of so many abusive relationships, does not get out of control and out of proportion. When jealousy enters a healthy relationship it does so proportionate to the experience. In the healthy relationship, there is room for other friends with few fears that the other friendships will minimize the dating relationship.

Trust also extends into what you choose to share with your date.

- Are you comfortable sharing your feelings?
- Do you trust that your date won't try to hurt you with something you shared with him?

Disclosing personal feelings or experiences from the past is risky. In a healthy relationship, you find that you want to share yourself because you trust your date to be as careful with your feelings as he is with his own. As the relationship continues, the trust grows based on your experiences together. Conversely, in an abusive relationship, trust diminishes because it has no way to flourish.

Mutually enjoyable sex

The sexual experience in a healthy relationship is equitable. It is mutually agreed upon and mutually enjoyed. If there are problems with sex, as there can be in many relationships, in the healthy relationship there is the opportunity to work it out.

This is not the case in abusive relationships. Sexual problems in these relationships usually are manifested in sexual abuse towards the woman. When the woman indicates that she's being hurt or isn't enjoying the sexual experience, she's generally not believed and often abused even more.

But in a healthy relationship, if the sex isn't good, at least it isn't abusive. And there's the possibility of working it out because the woman isn't afraid of being abused if she asks for something different.

Support

In a healthy relationship, the partners provide comfort and empathy to one another. Because they truly care about each other, each listens to what the other is saying—and often to what the other is not saying.

A couple that exudes support doesn't work at trying to reform each other. There's a realization that nobody's perfect and an acceptance of personal idiosyncrasies.

While annoyances do surface in any relationship, when mutual support enters a relationship, each person has his or her self-esteem conferred—not diminished. Support also means that you are there for each other during times of joy and times of pain: career change, loss of a family member, job promotion. You care about each other and what is happening in your lives. And it's not a one-way affair. He's just as concerned and supportive of you as you are of him.

Easygoing

In a healthy relationship, the overall tone is relaxed. You both have the ability to see the humorous side of life. You can laugh at yourselves without putting down one another. It's not humor at someone else's expense.

When your temperaments mesh and your styles are compatible, you recognize that there's an ease to the relationship which you may have missed in other less-healthy dating situations. You'll find that you aren't afraid to say what's on your mind, to suggest where to go on a date, or to comment on a world issue.

Often this sense of an easygoing relationship coincides with the lack of any physical aggression or threats of physical aggression. It may indicate that your feelings are being heard and you are being supported. In an abusive relationship, there's often a tenseness which centers on possible physical aggression, sexual abuse, or verbal and emotional abuse. The tenseness is there because you've recognized the potential for abuse or you've already been abused.

But when you're relaxed, you're confident that you'll remain intact, both physically and emotionally. In a healthy relationship you feel just as relaxed when you're together as when you're apart.

Fair fighting

Arguments, disagreements and issues surface in every relationship and when that occurs, it doesn't mean that the relationship is no longer healthy. Rather, in a healthy relationship, certain rules of fair fighting allow each person to come out the other end intact.

Rule 1 - No physical manifestations of power, no hitting, pushing, grabbing, shoving, kicking or beating up.

Rule 2 - Stay in the "here and now." The argument centers on what the issue is now, not the accumulation of annoyances from last year. The old stuff can be worked out later, not in the heat of heightened emotions. Instead, get in touch with why you are angry this time and talk that over with your partner.

Rule 3 - No name calling. Nothing is gained when names are flung around in an attempt to hurt your partner. Name-calling is a manipulation used to steer the argument away from the real issue. Instead, stay on the topic and talk about what you're feeling.

Rule 4 - Use "I" Statements. Saying what you feel, what you perceive, and what you need eliminates defensiveness on both of your parts.

In a healthy relationship, arguments don't have to be won or lost. Rather, healthy couples argue because they care about each other and they don't want things to build up and fester. Actually, couples who master the art of fighting fair usually can avoid many of the blow-up arguments that exist in relationships because they aren't afraid that the relationship will end with each argument. When the relationship is already built on respect, trust, mutually enjoyable sex and support, an argument or disagreement can be worked out because underlying all this are two people who truly care about one another.

Affirmation

The Dating Woman's Bill of Rights

Read this list aloud to yourself often. Believe what you're saying. And settle for nothing less than what you are entitled to. You have rights and you deserve them.

I have the right to trust myself above all others.
I have the right to decent treatment by anyone
I date.
I have the right to refuse to date anyone.
I have the right to be safe on a date.
I have the right to stop blaming myself
for dating abuse.
I have the right to be assertive on a date.
I have the right to pay my own way on a date.
I have the right to mutually consenting and
pleasurable sex.
I have the right to refuse to have sex.
I have the right to be respected as a person.
I have the right to disagree with my date.
I have the right to say *No*.
I have the right to get angry.

I have the right to fulfill myself with or without a
   man in my life.
I have the right to know who I am.
I have the right to know who I am dating.
I have the right to determine the criteria concerning
   who I will date.
I have the right to use my own transportation
   on a date.
I have the right to leave any dating situation
   my instincts tell me to.
I have the right to prosecute for battery and
   sexual assault.
I have the right to emotional support and
   understanding from others.
I have the right to a healthy dating relationship.
I have the right to control my own destiny.
I have the right to be selfish and get the good things
   I want from a relationship.
I have the right to be loved.
I have the right to be cared about.
I have the right to intimacy.
I have the right to high self-esteem.

I have the right to trust myself above all others.

Claudette McShane — *1988*

Action

How to Start a Support Group for Dating-Abuse Survivors

Dating-abuse survivors need to recognize that they aren't alone. One of the most effective ways of doing so is by joining a support group. These guidelines will show you how to find a group or if there is no existing group, how to start one.

Preliminaries in finding a support group

The first thing you'll want to know is if there's an existing group in your area which would be appropriate for you. You can find this out by checking your local newspaper for community activities and meetings open to the public. Some papers list times and places for groups such as Alcoholics Anonymous, Parents Anonymous, Single Parents and other self-help oriented support groups. If you don't know the reason for a group's existence, call and ask about it. Don't go to just any support group because it gives support. It may be focused on a topic unrelated to your needs.

While you're culling the papers, start calling women's and social service agencies. Ask them if they offer any support groups for women and if so, what is the focus of each group. Does it seem likely to fit your needs? If so, explain your situation and ask if you can join the group. Don't try to fit yourself into an existing group

179

for women and if so, what is the focus of each group. Does it seem likely to fit your needs? If so, explain your situation and ask if you can join the group. Don't try to fit yourself into an existing group that isn't appropriate to you. You may not get the support you need.

When you've exhausted all possibilities for finding an appropriate support group, consider starting one. You can do this two ways: on your own or with help from an agency.

If you don't feel comfortable with tackling the job yourself, call the agency you determined to be the best for you and ask if they would consider pulling this group together with your help. Make an appointment to talk with the staff and ask for what you need: a meeting space, money to run an ad, a trained facilitator, etc. Make a list of your needs before you go so that you are clear in what you are asking. Get a commitment from the agency on what they can do and when. If they can't give you an answer right away, ask when you can call them back to get an answer. Sometimes agencies have to check with directors or a board before starting a new project. Be sensitive to this, but at the same time don't compromise your need to get this group started.

If you want to start the group on your own, you'll need the following: a meeting place and time and publicity to generate people to come to the group.

The meeting place should be at a neutral site rather than in your own home because your home may make it appear that this is *your* group rather than a *shared* group. Also, attempting to rotate homes among group members makes it difficult to keep track of where the group is meeting. Instead, a location in a church, bank or school meeting room will give the group stability and an undisturbed atmosphere. Of course, if nothing can be found immediately, hold it in your home rather than not have the group at all. One of the group members may have access to a neutral location and this can be discussed at the first meeting.

Publicity may be an ad in the classifieds or a free listing in your newspaper, church bulletin or other publication which lists community events. Also, send a press release to the news editor of your local paper or radio or TV station; it may result in a short news article. If you're near a campus, you may also want to post signs with your announcement.

180

The classified ad can be a variation of this sample.

Warning! Dating May be Hazardous to Your Health

Have you been abused in a dating relationship? Been hurt physically, sexually, emotionally or verbally by someone you've dated? Want to meet other women who've been through it too? A support group is meeting at (location), on (date), at (time) o'clock. Anonymous and confidential. Come join us!

If you want to send a short press release to your local, college or free-shopper newspaper, radio or TV station, you may use this format. Be sure to double space the copy.

FOR IMMEDIATE RELEASE   (date)
     For more information
     Call: (your name)
     (your phone number)
     (Note to media: do not use this name in the media release.)

WARNING! DATING MAY BE HAZARDOUS TO YOUR HEALTH

A new support group is forming in (your city) for

women who've been abused by their dates. As many

as fifty percent of dating women suffer physical,

sexual, emotional or verbal abuse from their dating

partners. Until now there has been no avenue of help

for dating-abuse survivors.

On (date), the first Dating Abuse support group

181

will meet at (place), at (time). There is no fee. *(or)*

There will be a charge of $___ to cover expenses.

The support group is sponsored by (include name of agency). *(or)* The support group is being founded by (Include your name only if you're willing to go public!) a woman who herself has been abused and seeks the support of other women in the same situation.

This ongoing support group is a means for dating-abuse survivors to realize that they are not alone, are not to blame for being abused and can regain control of their lives. The support group is based on a nonjudgmental attitude. The women who attend will be assured anonymity and confidentiality.

Be prepared to give more information, even an interview, should someone from the media call you. Make it clear, however, if you don't want your name used.

The first meeting

Now that you have your publicity, you'll need to get ready for your first meeting.

If an agency is providing you with a facilitator, meet with her prior to the first meeting. Establish understanding and trust. Get to know who she is and let her know about you. The two of you should agree on the structure of the first meeting.

Having a trained facilitator can be helpful in several ways.

The facilitator is the person who sees that the group stays on track. Though not an actual group member herself, the facilitator has been trained in working with groups so that the group gets the most out of its existence.

The facilitator brings with her a background and knowledge about how people act in groups. She'll be able to handle the sticky situations which could arise, like a member who refuses to participate or one who tries to dominate. And because this is her role, she's usually given the latitude of saying things like, "Sharon, let's give Mary a chance to make her point."

The facilitator gives an extra assurance that the group commitment to being nonjudgmental, anonymous and confidential will be carried out. She's the one who initially will assert the rules of the group.

The group can be run without a trained facilitator if the members can commit to sharing the role of the facilitator. Actually, as a group progresses, the roles played by the facilitator become absorbed by its members. This is a sign that the group is working at its maximum potential.

My suggestion for the format of the initial support group meeting is the following:

- **State the purpose of the group.**

   To support women dating-abuse survivors in realizing that they are not alone, are not to blame for being abused, and that they can regain control of their lives.

- **State the premises of the group and the commitment each group member has to one another.**

   The support group is based on a nonjudgmental attitude. This means that my problems are no worse or better than your problems. We do not blame one another for what has happened or criticize each other. We also agree to not give advice unless a member specifically asks. The women who attend the group will be assured anonymity and confidentiality. First names only may be used and no member may discuss what anyone else has said in group to anyone outside of the group. Also, no one has to talk in the group if she doesn't want to.

- **Start rounds.**

Rounds are a way for a group to get started. I suggest that you use three questions for your initial rounds and that you begin first by stating
- Who you are,
- Why you're here, and
- What you want from this group.

Then turn to the person on your right or left and ask if she'd like to go next. Let each person talk in succession with the option of anyone to pass her turn. Depending on the time remaining, you may continue the discussion by asking how people feel right now. Again start with yourself by sharing your own feelings—scared, relieved, excited, energized.

Or you could ask each woman to state what she likes the best about herself and what she likes the least.

- **Establish group rules.**

Allow about 15 minutes for this portion of the meeting. Before the end of the first meeting, remember to establish the time and place for subsequent meetings. So you won't need to spend much time discussing rules, ask if the group will accept the following rules for now, which can be brought up for discussion and changed at a later date. A good length of time for a group is one-and-a-half hours.

- **Pass out a copy of the following:**

1. There will be total anonymity as to who is in the group. You may share first names only, if you choose. No one may disclose the names of who is in the group.

2. The group and its members agree to be nonjudgmental towards one another. There will be no blaming and no criticism.

3. There will be no smoking or eating during group. Many people are bothered by smoke and no member should be subjected to second-hand smoke which could prevent her from continuing in the group. Food is a distraction to giving total attention to the group. The group can decide if it wants to have coffee, tea or soft drinks available.

4. The group will start promptly and end promptly. This respects the time set aside for the group and indicates the importance the group has in your lives.

5. Group members may socialize afterwards and members may take turns bringing snacks.

6. Each member is equally responsible for the success of the group.

7. Each member agrees to contact someone in the group or the facilitator if she no longer will be attending.

• **When you've established these initial rules and everyone agrees to them, you can close the group by asking each person what they got out of the meeting.**

On-going group process

Subsequent groups can focus on issues or topics which the members predetermine. Or the group can function in a less organized manner and start each meeting with rounds and an indication of what members need from the group that night. Generally this less structured method is best run by a trained facilitator because it is more likely to get off the track and to miss the needs of some of its members.

- Some topics or issues which members may decide to discuss may include

    Self-blame
    Sexism
    Alcohol and drugs
    Pornography and its support of dating abuse
    Methods of healing
    Warning signs
    Prevention
    Women's power
    Men's power
    Women's intuition
    Dating myths
    Old beliefs/New beliefs about dating
    Date rape
    Women's feelings of inadequacy
    Self-esteem
    The media's promotion of dating abuse
    Childhood and growing up female
    Elements of a healthy relationship

Before you close the group, ask if more members are needed and if more publicity should be generated to bring in new members. Usually a group of ten to twelve members is ideal. If the group is larger, it will be difficult for everyone to talk during group time. If it's smaller than six, you'll lose some of the power which is generated from its larger membership.

Enjoy your group and the support, encouragement and enlightenment it brings to your life. You deserve it!

About the author
Claudette McShane

Claudette McShane, M.S.W., helped develop the first shelter for battered women in Milwaukee, Wisconsin, in 1978. Over 20,000 women and children were served through the shelter and hotline which she headed as executive director for six years. She also directed Batterers Anonymous, a self-help group program for abusive men.

In 1981, she received a Women-Helping-Women award from the Soroptimists, an international professional women's organization. She was one of ten women worldwide to receive this distinction.

She has published articles on family violence in professional journals such as *Social Work* and the *California Sociologist*, and in *Mothering, Youth!* and *Campus Life* magazines; served on the Governor's Task Force on Domestic Abuse; led workshops; been an assistant professor of social work; lectured at universities and presented at various national and local conferences. She also has served on the boards of directors of numerous social service agencies.

In 1986, McShane received a grant from the American Association of University Women's Educational Foundation to complete work on the manuscript of *Warning! Dating May Be Hazardous to Your Health!*

McShane also served in the Peace Corps in Brazil.

Mother Courage Press

In addition to *Warning! Dating may be hazardous to your health!*, Mother Courage Press also publishes

Fear or Freedom, a Woman's Options in Social Survival and Physical Defense by Susan E. Smith. *Library Journal* in its March 1, 1987 issue highly recommended *Fear or Freedom* and called it "an important new approach to self-defense for women." Using the results of a four-part research project on rape, assault and successful resistance stories involving 209 women and her nine years of study in the martial arts, the author has developed a strategy that involves situational advantages, interaction, inter-personal dynamics, attack styles and all degrees of confrontation. She shows why and how known-assailant rape is the most preventable and easiest to defend against. Women today need answers—not admonitions. The book realistically offers options to fear of social intimidation and fear of violent crime.
Paperback, Illustrated, 8 1/2 by 11, (224 pages) $11.95

Why Me? Help for victims of child sexual abuse (even if they are adults now) by Lynn B. Daugherty. This book was written to be read by survivors of child sexual abuse who are now teenagers or adults. It is also intended for counselors or other people who want to understand and help these survivors. It was chosen for the Editors Choice Award for Young Adults in 1986 by the American Library Association's publication, *booklist*. Its reviewer wrote, "Emphasizing the responsibility of the abuser, the fact that abuse is a widespread experience, and the dynamics of an abusive situation, Daugherty begins the process of healing psychological wounds."
Paperback, (112 pages) $7.95

Rebirth of Power, Overcoming the Effects of Sexual Abuse through the Experiences of Others edited by Pamela Portwood, Michele Gorcey and Peggy Sanders. This book seeks to shatter the silence which preserves and condones sexual violence in our society and to break the stereotypes and illusions surrounding sexual assualt. It is an anthology of poetry and prose providing space for those most qualified to address these issues and to share the knowledge they have gained at painful prices.
Paperback, (208 pages) $9.95

Something Happened to Me by Phyllis Sweet. This is a sensitive, straightforward book designed to help children victimized by incest or other sexual abuse. A reviewer for *Young Children, the Official Journal of the National Association for the Education of Young Children,* wrote, "The marvelous introduction and epilogue are written for adults and reveal the extraordinary care that the author, a school psychologist, has taken to assure the dignity and self-worth of children from troubled families."
Paperback, Illustrated, 8 1/2 by 11, (36 pages) $4.95

Watch for more healing and helping books, novels, biographies and poetry with a feminist perspective from Mother Courage Press.

If you don't find them in your local book store, you may order books directly from Mother Courage Press at 1533 Illinois Street, Racine, WI 53405. Please add $1.50 for postage and handling for the first book and $.25 for each additional book.